Midget

by
TIM
BOWLER

ALADDIN PAPERBACKS
New York London Toronto Sydney Singapore

First Aladdin Paperbacks edition June 2000
First published in England 1994 by Oxford University Press, Oxford

Copyright © 1994 by Tim Bowler

Aladdin Paperbacks
An imprint of Simon & Schuster
Children's Publishing Division
1230 Avenue of the Americas
New York, NY 10020

Also available in a Margaret K. McElderry Books hardcover edition.

Book design by Ann Bobco
The text for this book was set in Perpetua

Printed and bound in the United States of America

10 9 8 7 6 5 4 3 2 1

The Library of Congress has cataloged the hardcover edition as follows:

Bowler, Tim.
Midget / Tim Bowler.—1st U.S. ed.
p.   cm.
Summary: Subject to strange fits, physically abnormal, and psychologically disturbed from the constant torment and abuse of his older brother, fifteen-year-old Midget finds himself in control of his life for the first time when he gets his own sailboat and discovers untapped mental powers.
ISBN 0-689-80115-7 (hc.)
[1. Physically handicapped—Fiction. 2. Brothers—Fiction. 3. Emotional problems—Fiction.
4. Boats and boating—Fiction. 5. Extrasensory perception—Fiction.] I. Title.
PZ.B6786Mi 1995
[Fic]—dc20
ISBN 0-689-82909-4 (Aladdin pbk.)

To Rachel, with love

Mind is the Masterpower that moulds and makes,
And Man is Mind, and evermore he takes
The tool of Thought, and shaping what he wills,
Brings forth a thousand joys, a thousand ills:
He thinks in secret, and it comes to pass:
Environment is but his looking-glass.

James Allen

One

The voice hissed into his ear.

"So you managed to sneak out again. And have another lit-tle look at what you know you can't have. What a pointless exercise."

There was no need to turn to know who it was. No need to try and run.

No point in running.

He'd been wondering if maybe this could be his year. The year everything worked out right, even though it was half gone and nothing was changed. And he'd been daring to dream. About the usual thing.

But that tumbled out of his mind now. In its place came thoughts of pain, fear, darkness.

"You know you shouldn't be here," sneered the voice. "You should be at home, getting ready for your"– the sarcasm deepened– "big appointment."

He blinked hard, knowing what was coming, feeling it starting to slither over his mind and body, somehow laughing at his useless attempts to hold it back. But already the estu-ary was receding. For a moment he saw the glistening belly of mud, and far out from the shore, the waters of the Ray Gut, dancing with boats. Even the dark, distant shape of Southend Pier, stretched out like an uncurled whip. Then that faded with the rest.

"Vision going?" The voice clucked in mock sympathy. "Usually does, doesn't it? You mustn't get so worked up over things."

He felt his fingers twist and clutch around his eyes, as though trying to hold in the light that now oozed from them. High above him, he heard gulls screaming.

The voice gave an exaggerated sigh, this time in his other ear. "Another fit coming. And here you are, with just me to look after you."

"A-Ah!" A tremor rippled through his hands, and he thrust them into his pockets.

"That won't work," jeered the voice. "You won't stop the spasms that way. You've tried that before."

Now all he saw was darkness. In the absence of light, he clung to other sensations: the tang of the estuary; the prickle of sweat along his neck; the rumble of a train behind the seawall, thundering down toward Southend. But these, too, were leaving him. He felt his head roll, his eyes gyrate, his shoulders, arms, legs tense and twitch. He tasted blood on his tongue where he'd bitten it.

The voice came back again, drawling its favorite theme.

"Midget. Mad Midget. The loony from Leigh-on-Sea."

"M-m-m—" The first spasm locked him in a knot of pain.

"Midget the Mumbler. Fifteen years old. And he still can't master his speech impediment. Not that we want to hear him talk."

He managed to champ his jaws, but whether to spit or snarl or bite, he no longer knew, nor could control.

"Midget the Masher. Who can't eat without getting food all over himself. And everybody else."

"M-m—"

"Midget the Moron. Can't read the simplest word or write his own name. No wonder they won't have him at school. And hardly surprising the home tutors keep giving up."

"M—"

"Midget the Mess. Acne all over. And three feet tall!"

"M—"

Now the voice was a guffaw. "Midget the Mistake. The ugly little dwarf who turned up even though we never wanted him."

Suddenly it lowered. "Midget the Murderer."

"M-m—"

And hardened. "My pathetic little brother."

There were no more words, and none were needed. He would not have heard them anyway. The spasms had taken over and could not be stopped. He fell back, gasping for air, as the fit rushed upon him like a smothering sea.

I'm not a murderer. It was an accident. I never meant . . .

He looked around him at the bright timbered room, with its newly waxed surfaces and general air of prosperity, and ran his finger over the shiny leather arm of the chair. Then he leaned back. He was tired, and not just from the journey here.

He wondered who had carried him home from the seafront. But he could guess the answer, and it only increased his resentment.

I'm not a murderer. It was an accident.

He scowled down at the body he hated, and thought how good it would be to murder that, if he knew he could replace it with a decent one.

I hate you, he said to it. I hate you almost as much as I hate the name Midget, and the person who gave it to me, as his secret, personal insult word—the only person who knows it, and uses it. When no one else is around, of course.

Apart from Ned. But Ned's just a sheep. Ned'll never do anything on his own.

He managed to stop the left hand from shaking.

Now even I call myself Midget. I've gotten so used to hearing it from him. I've almost forgotten my real name.

He concentrated on the right hand, and finally stopped that from shaking, too. But the left had started again.

There's only one person who understands anything about me. And she only knows a bit. She doesn't know about the worst part. But I suppose she's bound to have a blind spot in that direction.

He glowered out of the window at the dirty street. He hated coming to London, just to see some new, bloodless specialist. And especially as this had turned out to be a drought year. Even with the fan on, he could feel his shirt sticking to him. He watched the sun bouncing off the tops of the cars as they sped past, and wished he were back at Leigh, looking over the estuary.

I'm supposed to have the world at my feet. But it's the other way around. The world's got me at its feet.

He lifted his gaze above the cars and into the sky, and as always happened when he did this, the sky became the sea, and he found himself thinking of the dream. The dream they told him he could never have.

The thing he wanted almost as much as being normal. Almost as much as being revenged.

Maybe more.

Voices sounded in the corridor, and he looked toward the door. Dad's was always easy to recognize: cheerful, well-meaning, garrulous, and not aware in the slightest of how easily it carried. The other voice was new. But he could guess.

8

"He's a terrific boy," Dad was saying. "Most people don't realize what a super kid he is. Great sense of humor. But you've got to be patient with him. He gets very uptight. He's trying to express himself all the time, and he doesn't always do it right. I mean, he doesn't do it in the normal way. So people get the wrong end of the stick. Smiling, for example. When he smiles, it can look a bit grotesque, and it puts some people off. But you've got to be understanding. You've just got to try and figure out what he means. I'm sure, you know, with the right help, he could—"

"Mmm." The other voice cut him off with a long, smooth purr; but whether the purr was from sympathy, or just a desire to stop the flow of chatter, was difficult to know. Then it spoke. "Bearing in mind his physical problems, it's hardly surprising to find him psychologically disadvantaged."

Not an unpleasant voice, he decided. A bit musical, in fact. But also cool, unemotional, and very sure of itself. He tried to imagine the face that would go with it.

The door swung open, and he looked up. Wrong again. Nothing like he expected, and certainly very different from Dad's, which was craggy and tanned, with the big smile, a feature of his inability to see the evil in anyone, chiseled in its usual position.

The other face was older by a good ten years, and judging by the pallor of the long cheeks, the man was not very healthy. And there was something clinical about the way the eyes moved, as though studying a specimen in a jar. But at least he held out his hand.

"I'm Dr. Patterson," he said. "I'm a psychiatrist. I expect your father's explained things to you."

Midget looked at his father, who colored slightly. "I . . . haven't actually spoken to him much about this." Dad headed for the other armchair. "Except to say we were

9

coming to meet you. To see if . . . you know, you can—"

"Throw some light on these fits," said the psychiatrist, sitting down at the desk. Midget found the eyes studying him again, and he stared back, expecting them to turn away. But they went on, quietly, patiently analyzing, as though in a reverie. It didn't seem unfriendly, so he tried to decide whether or not to risk one of his smiles on the man.

Maybe not just yet. Most people thought his smiles were snarls, unless they already knew him. But something had to be done, either to puncture the man's unending concentration or just to be friendly back. He decided on a calculated wink.

It was definitely a mistake. The man looked away at once as though he'd had ink flicked in his face. And now he was shuffling the papers on his desk, pretending to look for something.

Midget shrugged, disappointed, and winked at Dad instead, who winked back. But Dad always winked back.

"Now then." The psychiatrist looked over at Dad. "This is only an exploratory session, as I explained to you on the phone, and to start with, I need to ask you some questions. Your son and I will have plenty of time to get to know each other in future sessions."

Midget looked sharply at Dad.

Future sessions? I don't like the sound of that. I thought this was a one-time thing.

Dad caught his glance but only said, "Fair enough. What do you want to know?"

"Well, there's quite a lot of information in the file about his physical difficulties. But I want to know more about these attacks."

The psychiatrist put on a pair of glasses and went on, leafing through the file as he spoke. "The various specialists you have consulted, and your general practitioner, all appear to incline to the view that the fits are not necessarily what one might refer to as . . . epileptic. I believe you have discussed this already?"

"Yes. The last person we saw—the one who suggested we come to you—he thought—"

"That the fits might be related to some kind of emotional disturbance, yes. A state of anxiety, for instance. Can you recall his first attack?"

Dad frowned. "He's had so many of them now, it's difficult to remember exactly when they started. He always seems to have had them."

I remember the first attack, Midget thought. I remember every attack. Every single one.

"But I think it must have been around the age of six or seven. I do remember one in the garden, early on, a really awful one."

It wasn't that one. I'd had lots by then, only you never knew. The first one was long before that. He came in the darkness, as usual. But it was the first time he did more than just taunt me.

"And how do they start?"

"Well, that's the worrying thing. They seem to affect him when he's on his own."

No. No. No.

"Your son's shaking his head." The psychiatrist looked over briefly, then back to Dad.

Dad frowned. "He's probably thinking about Seb."

Midget nodded violently, and Dad frowned again.

"Seb?" said the psychiatrist.

"His brother."

"Older? Younger?"

"Older. Seventeen. Lives for sailing, like me and the boy here. Not surprising, really. I've been taking them out in *Trade Wind* since the day they were born."

"*Trade Wind?*"

"My cabin cruiser."

"Ah."

Midget looked out at the sky, and instantly the dream came back. He knew Dad was watching him, and would guess what was in his mind. The psychiatrist's voice broke in again.

"So you're all sailing enthusiasts? Your wife, too?"

Midget turned quickly back, in time to see Dad flush. "My wife died some years ago."

Fifteen years ago. Why don't you say it?

The psychiatrist gave a small cough. "I beg your pardon. Well, this brother, Seb. What does he do?"

"Apart from sailing?"

The psychiatrist gave the ghost of a smile. "Apart from sailing."

"He's just left school. He's waiting to go to college in the autumn."

The psychiatrist took off his glasses. "So why did you say, 'He's probably thinking about Seb'?"

"Did I say that?" Dad shifted in his seat. "Well, it's just that the boy's got a bit of a thing about his older brother. Doesn't seem to like him. Don't know why. Neither does Seb."

Midget wriggled around in the chair, determined to stop the twitching in his hands and face but powerless to do so. He looked at Dad and thought, you don't see what's been going on because you're too good and he's too clever.

"I just don't get it," Dad said, scratching his head. "Seb does his best—again and again—to be friendly. If you could see how caring he is. Totally supportive. But the boy still hates the sight of him."

Dad, Dad, Dad.

His father glanced at him. "It's no good you looking at me like that. Everyone else loves Seb. They can't all be wrong. Seb treats you very well. But you're always gunning for him."

Midget groaned and shuffled to the other side of the chair. He noticed the psychiatrist studying him again.

I can guess what you're thinking. Nice seventeen-year-old boy, loved by all, and ugly little midget brother, with chip on his shoulder. Because he's jealous.

He looked out of the window again, and called the dream back to his mind. Or perhaps it floated to him of its own accord, or had been there all the time, and did not have to come back. He no longer knew. It was there so often now. In his mind he saw the cobbled street of Old Leigh; he was alone, and he wandered down to Bell Wharf, and stood gazing at the water below him, ebbing eastward toward Southend Pier, and out to the open sea. And as his mind watched, the personality of the estuary changed: The tide slid back, and the vast inshore mud bank opened up, and he watched it for a while, almost smelling its soft, salty wetness; then his eyes roamed out from the shore, a mile or so, to the South Bank, stretching toward the darker, deeper body of the Thames, and the shores of Kent. Then they came back to the thing that fascinated him most: the ever-fluent channel of the Ray Gut, wriggling between the two banks like a huge eel.

He wanted to linger in the Ray, but the moving waters seemed to sweep his mind on, eastward, past the Low-Way Buoy at the mouth of the Gut, and away from the South Bank, until he saw the end of Southend Pier rising before him. The dream darkened at this point.

"I'll give you another example."

The sound of Dad's voice reminded him with a start that the two men had been talking all the time.

"He had an attack this morning, down at Old Leigh. He's not supposed to be out on his own. He gets so many fits now, it could be dangerous."

Dad wiped the sweat from his forehead.

"Anyway, he did go off, without telling anyone. We guessed where he was. And who went looking for him, and literally had to carry him back? Seb. And just as well. He couldn't have walked."

Midget looked down at his body, squirming around in the chair, and tried to force it to be still. Dad always talked his feelings aloud, whether to psychiatrist, newspaper boy, or next-door's cat, whoever came along first. There was never any anger. But it didn't make it any easier to take.

"One day you'll appreciate Seb's qualities," Dad said. "And when you do, I think you'll feel ashamed of the way you've behaved to him all these years."

Midget gripped the arms of the chair to stop himself from falling off.

The psychiatrist was studying them both now, but it was hard to know what he was thinking. Then he looked at his watch.

"Well, let's see what effect the treatment has on your son."

Midget whirled around at Dad in alarm.

You never said anything about treatment.

He followed Dad sullenly out of the clinic, down the streets and into the subway station.

"I know what you're thinking," said Dad. "But don't worry. It won't hurt. It might do some good." His father stopped at the token booth. "To be honest, I didn't tell you beforehand because I thought you might run away again."

Right, I would have.

"And I really wanted you to meet Dr. Patterson first. I felt sure you'd trust him. He's a nice man, isn't he?"

Midget looked away. You lied. You said we were just going to have a talk.

"It won't start right away. He'll want to ask more questions. And I'll be with you all the time."

14

They made their way to the platform and waited, hemmed in by jostling bodies, though from his level, all he saw was legs and attaché cases. The train rattled in, more bodies poured out, and the fight started for places. Somehow Dad found two seats together.

"I'll stay with you during the treatment, too, if you like," he whispered.

Midget glared at him, but it was no use. He never could be really angry with Dad. He heard giggling nearby, and saw two girls watching him and nudging each other. As if this were a cue, eyes turned toward him from the other seats, looking him over with unashamed fascination. He swept a snarling glance around them all.

But the scrutiny continued, until finally his father noticed. "Sorry, did anybody have a question?" he said, looking around. "Did somebody want to ask something?" Dad always resorted to a mild sarcasm when this happened; it was the nearest he ever came to confronting people.

The eyes lowered, but the curiosity of others returned the moment they left the subway at Tower Hill. Glances stalked him predatorily, reminding him with every passerby that his face was ugly and strange, his body repellent, the twists and twitches in his movements both comical and disturbing.

He had known the stares all his life. He had never known how to stop them from hurting him.

Yet the picture of the dream came back to him, despite the stares, and stayed with him as they climbed aboard the train at Fenchurch Street Station and set off back to Leigh-on-Sea. He closed his eyes and gave it his full attention. As they pulled out, he heard Dad's voice in his ear.

"I can guess what you're thinking about, now that we're going home." There was a pause, and he heard the whine of the train as it accelerated. "I can't stop you from having a dream. I want you to have dreams. But this one . . ." Another pause. "Look, will you at least promise me you won't run off today to have another look at it? Just for today. Promise?"

He nodded, without opening his eyes. It would probably be too late anyway when they got back, so it was an easy promise to make.

He felt Dad shuffle slightly, and knew there would be more words. Having had variations of this conversation so often, he knew what to expect.

"I hate to keep on about this . . ." Dad said.

But you feel you've got to.

"But I feel I've got to."

You can't have it. You know why. I'm sorry.

"It's not that I want to stop you from having things. But this particular thing you want—well, you know why you can't have it. It could be dangerous for you. I just don't want you to be at risk." Midget felt a hand on his arm, then heard a quiet "Sorry, son."

The touch left his arm, and he felt Dad lean back. He kept his eyes closed and watched the dream unfold in his mind, a dream far too powerful to resist, despite what Dad and others said. Not that he wanted to resist it. When he finally opened his eyes, forty minutes had passed; he saw Dad asleep on his left, and the estuary to the right, sparkling like a diamond. The train started to brake, and the long wall of Chalkwell Station appeared, cutting off his view of the water.

Dad stirred and grunted. "We here?"

Midget nodded. They made their way out of the station and up the hill, the late afternoon sun still hot enough to be uncomfortable. Multicolored sails littered the estuary, and Midget gazed and wished.

Dad nudged him. "You did promise, remember."

They came over the brow of the hill, and headed on toward the little alleyway leading to Woodfield Gardens.

He thought, I remember the promise. But it only makes me remember the dream more.

He thought of it all evening, until it mastered him so strongly that he forgot everything else: the treatment, the stares of the passersby earlier, his body.

Even Seb.

Until later.

At the approach of night, the dream vanished, and fear reclaimed him. Dad's light went out, the house grew dark and still; he lay on his bed and stared up at the ceiling, and waited in dread.

He knew it was useless to try and stop the gnawing in his stomach, the twitching in his hands, the cascade of thoughts through his mind, each one a mirror of hideous expectancy for what might come. He heard the moan of a car at the other end of Woodfield Gardens, then the sound receded, and silence returned, and lasted so long that he almost dared to think he might be spared tonight. Then he heard the twist of the doorknob.

The barricade didn't work. There was a soft grating sound, as the chairs dug under the carpet before falling noiselessly back against the side of the bed. The books he had spent so long piling on top slid to the floor.

The shadow loomed over him.

He heard a chuckle, then the big hand locked onto his throat and forced out his breath. He squirmed, gasping for air, praying it would only be taunts and threats tonight, not the unspeakable alternative.

He was lucky. And the shadow stayed only an hour.

But the words whispered into his ear did not go.

"You killed her, Mad Midget. You killed her. And I'm going to kill you. Before the summer's out."

two

"Plates! Quick! Under the broiler!"

He hurried over to the stove and felt them with the tips of his fingers.

"They shouldn't be that hot." Dad bustled around the kitchen, as though making sausage and bacon for breakfast required a maximum expenditure of energy. But the smell wafting from the frying pan was good. Cooking was not Dad's strong point, yet for some reason, sausage and bacon usually came out right.

He pulled out the plates and stood by the kitchen window for a moment. Looking out, he saw a house martin flit past and away over the apple trees in the garden. It was already growing hot. He thought of the estuary, only minutes away.

"Stick the plates on the side there."

He watched Dad capering over the frying pan. It was always comical when Dad cooked. Dad caught his eye and grinned. "You needn't look at me like that. I may be lacking in finesse, but I'm still the head chef around here."

Midget gave his crazy, distorted grin, which only a few people recognized for what it was. Fortunately, Dad was one of them. Then he noticed something he would have to tell Dad about before much longer. He raised his arm to point, then changed his mind; that was too easy.

"M-m-m–" he said, waving the arm in circles instead.

Dad looked down at him. "What, now? You want to . . .?" He was halfway through scraping the sausage and bacon onto the plates. "All right, if it's a quick one."

Midget held up a finger.

"One word."

He held the finger to his arm.

"One syllable." Dad was watching intently, the frying pan poised over the table. Midget went on through the game, relishing Dad's boyish enjoyment every time they did this.

"Sounds like, sounds like . . . come on, sounds like what?"

Midget looked about him wildly. Then it came, and he pointed.

"Eyes? Sounds like eyes? Right. Ties . . . guys . . . pies . . ."

Midget jumped up and down.

"Dies . . . lies . . ."

Midget stuck out his arms. They were meant to look like wings, but Dad thought he was pointing out of the window.

"Skies!" he shouted.

"M-m-m–" Midget shook his head, and started to race about the kitchen, his arms still outstretched. Dad started laughing.

"Tries!" he bellowed. "It's rugby. You're playing rugby!" His face was bright with triumph. Midget started laughing, too, and saw Dad's expression cloud. "It's not rugby. It's something else."

Midget flopped into the chair, giggling. It was good being with Dad. He was just thinking of something else he could do to convey the word, when he realized that the muscles all over his body were tightening.

He didn't need to look around. The early warning signals were so reliable, after years of practice, that he never doubted them. He knew, without seeing or hearing, that his brother was near.

Seb was behind him, standing in the doorway, the big smile enveloping them both.

"Morning, guys. How's everybody?"

"Confused." Dad was still chuckling. "He's doing a charade and I can't get it."

"Let me see it. You obviously need some help." Seb nodded toward the window. "That flypaper's disgusting. It's covered with flies."

"I'll put a new one up after we've cracked this charade. Right, let's try it again."

But Midget could only shake his head. It seemed unfair that Seb, who purposely caused him so much pain, could even spoil things by accident. His father was still watching, waiting for some explanation. Midget did his impression of wings again, then pointed.

Suddenly Dad understood, and burst out laughing.

"What's up?" said Seb.

"Tell you later. Let's eat."

They started breakfast, and he tried to ignore the tightness in his muscles that he always felt in Seb's presence, even when others were around.

"You're up a bit late this morning," Dad said to Seb.

"Slept like a log. No dreams, nothing."

"Must have a clear conscience."

"Yup." Seb turned to Midget. "You sleep okay?"

Midget had been trying not to dribble, but felt saliva on his chin, mixed with chewed sausage and bacon. He clapped the napkin to his face, and saw that his hand was knotted into a fist. But Seb merely smiled in the friendliest manner, then turned to Dad.

"And you reckon this psychiatrist might be able to help?"

"He seems reasonable. And he was highly recommended. He's certainly clever. There's hardly room on his business card for all the letters after his name."

"So he's expensive?"

Dad wiped a piece of bread around his plate. "I don't give a damn what it costs."

Midget looked up at him, remembering his earlier response to the idea of treatment, and felt ashamed. Dad meant well and had worries enough of his own, with the chandlery shop in Leigh struggling. Midget thought of the paint peeling off the window frames of their house, the garage roof that still leaked, the fence that had blown down in the March gales and still hadn't been mended—all things that a practical, competent person would do something about. And Dad was both practical and competent. But he was seldom at home now; he was always at the shop. Which meant long hours when Seb could do what he liked.

He saw his brother glance over and wink. "Let's hope the psychiatrist can do something. We're all rooting for you, kid."

Dad was pouring coffee. "You racing today?"

"'Course."

"What's the tally with Ned so far this season?"

"Up 'til last week he had three wins and I had three. But I won yesterday, and he capsized. So I'm ahead."

Dad shrugged. "You should be beating Ned anyway. You're a much better helmsman. And your boat's a flier, especially off the wind."

"Well, he's my only real rival at the club."

"And he's no rival at all. You going across the road after breakfast?"

"She's coming here."

Midget sat up straight, unable to stop himself. Seb gave the flicker of a glance in his direction.

"What time's she coming?" said Dad.

"Ten minutes ago."

"Nice of you to tell us."

As Dad spoke, there was a knock at the back door. Midget quickly wiped his mouth and hands, and tried to keep his eyes on the food still to be eaten. But already through the glass of the door, he could see the slender outline, the silhouetted mane of hair that tumbled thickly down to the waist. He sensed his brother's eyes on him again.

Dad opened the door.

"Hello, Jenny. Come for this oaf, have you?"

"'Fraid so." She came over to the table and sat by Seb. "What time do you want to go?"

Seb glanced at his watch. "No hurry. Race isn't for ages yet. No water in anyway. But we can wander down now if you want."

"I don't mind so long as I get some sun."

"Glad you're giving yourself a break," said Dad. "You certainly need one."

"Mom thinks I'm practicing too much."

"She's right. Every time I go past your house I hear you scraping that fiddle. Not that it doesn't sound impressive. What have you got coming up?"

"Big competition. I just qualify for the under-sixteens."

"What piece are you playing?"

Midget felt the word come from deep within himself, so violently that he almost choked on his food.

"Br-Br-Brah—" he stammered, unable to say more. But somehow he knew Jenny had understood.

She bent down and looked him hard in the face. "Were you trying to say 'Brahms'? You were, weren't you?"

He nodded.

"It is Brahms. How did you know? I haven't told any of you, not even Seb."

He felt himself flush, not only because of her sudden attention, but because he didn't know the answer himself.

Dad gave a laugh. "He must be psychic."

"Maybe he is," said Jenny.

Seb stood up. "Come on, let's go."

Jenny still looked confused, and Midget knew she wanted to talk more about it. But she stood up, too. Dad leaned back in his chair and beamed up at Seb.

"What it is to have a girlfriend come and watch you race. Never happened to me."

"Still could. You're not that old."

"Very funny."

Seb gave his winning smile. "Some of us have got it, some of us haven't." Again Midget noted the flicker of the eyes toward him. He knew what it meant and scowled back. But the smile seemed to engulf him, as it engulfed them all.

The moment they had gone, Dad turned to him. "So, what are your plans?"

But Midget was already halfway out the back door.

I must see it. I must.

He hung around the road for a while, hiding behind parked cars until Seb and Jenny had disappeared down the path at the bottom of Woodfield Gardens. Then he raced after them. Seb wouldn't do anything to him with Jenny there. That would come later. But first . . .

First the dream. The dream, no matter what.

He spotted them at the top of the Undercliff, holding hands, looking over the estuary, but more important, standing still. He scuttled along the top side of the road as fast as he could, keeping a wary eye upon them. They didn't turn, but somehow he sensed Seb knew he was there, and would guess at once where he was going. But that didn't alter things for now.

I'm going to make it. Nothing can stop me.

He slipped across the road and down to the bridge that spanned the railway line. From there he gazed over the estuary, still hard and dry, though the Creek and Ray Gut were swelling fast as the flood tide gobbled the land. But there was no time to linger here. He hurried down to the Cinder Path and along toward Old Leigh.

The stares of passersby bothered him less down here; there was always so much he wanted to look at. Today he hardly noticed them. All he saw was the racing dinghies.

Especially the Leigh-on-Sea One-Designs.

Among them Seb's. He stared at the little boat, still neat in its cover, and at all the others, some half rigged already, and one even at the base of the slipway ready to be launched. There were several helmsmen at the rack already, and the usual air of confidence hung around them. It would be replaced by awe when Seb arrived.

The thought of his brother not far behind made him put on speed. The dinghy rack dropped away, and he was soon close to Bell Wharf and the approaches to Old Leigh. Now the glances of others did intrude, as he dodged around legs and strollers and bags. But at last the Cinder Path widened and he squeezed along to the right, keeping away from the beach with its jaunty throng of visitors, and at last that, too, dropped away, and he was on the main street of Old Leigh, excitement growing within him.

I've made it, I've made it.

He knew his face twitched with pleasure, attracting even more attention, but he didn't care. He ran past the café, past the shop, past the bar, and didn't stop running until he was there.

No need to peep through the crack in the door today. It was open. He could sit in his usual spot and gaze uninterruptedly at his dream. He climbed onto the barrel, swung his legs around until he was comfortable, and looked into the boatyard.

The dinghy lay close by, propped up in its usual place by the entrance, the bow pointed straight toward him, as though to welcome the only person in the world who seemed to care about it anymore. Week after week since he'd first noticed it, he'd asked himself why the hull had been immaculately half painted and then abandoned, why a boat that had been built so beautifully had been left unfinished, why it wasn't already sold and out racing with the other Leigh-on-Sea One-Designs like Seb's.

Why it couldn't be his.

He looked around the yard at the workers. He knew them all by sight, having been there so often, and they seemed to accept him now. Sometimes the foreman even nodded to him. But they were always busy, and he couldn't stammer out his questions anyway.

But he could dream, and as always happened when he sat here, the half-born boat became a full-grown boat in his mind, the painting and varnishing complete, buoyancy bags and centerboard and rudder all in place, and the sail bent on the boom, and then the boat would plunge out through the water with him at the helm, away from the shore, away from pain. And today the dream seemed so strong that the five hours he sat there passed like a minute, and it was with a start of dismay that he remembered that the real world was not like the dream, and he would have to go back to it.

He found them waiting for him at the rack.

He'd thought it would be safe to go back along the Cinder Path, that the race wouldn't be over yet, and anyway, Jenny would be around.

But Jenny was nowhere to be seen, and most of the boats were back. He edged along, wishing the crowds that had jostled around him before were still there. But he had stayed at the boatyard longer than he intended, and the afternoon was drawing on. He crouched slightly, to take full advantage of his smallness, and crept closer to the rack.

He saw figures moving around, the sailing set in force, fawning as usual around Seb, who was bent over *Scorpion*'s dark blue hull at the top of the slipway.

Seb the leader. The magnet, the legend. The best junior helmsman in the club. The youngest person ever to win the Nore Race. The hero, hailed by newspaper and national TV, who at thirteen had brought *TradeWind* back single-handed to Leigh from halfway across the English Channel, through some of the roughest seas many could remember, with Dad sprawled in agony around the cabin in the grip of an angina attack, and he—Midget—too young, too small, too frightened to do more than shake.

Seb, the big attraction. The charismatic, friendly guy, who'd help anyone with a problem.

Midget drew closer and heard laughs; Seb was cracking jokes, and everyone was happy. He lowered his head and scampered forward.

No one looked his way. He reached the low fence that bordered the rack and crouched there, breathing hard. Then, still keeping low, he slipped along the outside, watching the flash of dark blue through each gap in the posts. To his relief, he was soon past. He straightened up to run the final leg toward the bridge and safety.

"So, it's Midget the Mouse!"

He looked up in dismay at the huge body blocking his way, and the leering, freckly face.

He'd forgotten about Ned.

"Seb said you always come back this way after your little trips." Ned's cheeks were creased in a puffy smile. "Asked me to look out for you."

Seb was still bent over the boat, the group around him as before, talking, laughing. Ned called out. "Seb!"

He saw faces turn toward him, and shrank back.

I won't get hurt. Not here. Not with all these people around. Not with—

He felt the metal of the railway fence dig into his back. Ned called out again, and added, "There's someone to see you."

Now Seb was sauntering over, a long piece of rope in his hands, and as he walked, he coiled it slowly and very deliberately, and smiled. And Midget knew that to anyone else, it was the smile of delight at seeing the much-loved younger brother, a smile so convincing and so practiced that even Ned looked surprised for a moment, and somewhat disappointed. Seb stopped at the low fence, and leaned there for a moment, and watched them without a word; then suddenly, he vaulted over onto the Cinder Path.

"M-m—" Midget spluttered and tried to worm his way along the fence, but both ways were now blocked. Seb edged closer, and still Midget felt the smile wash over him, so warm, so persuasive, that even he found himself wondering, mad though he knew it was, if for once it could be for real. The big, brotherly arm stretched over him protectively,

27

without quite touching him; the face came down close to his, the eyes shining affectionately. Still smiling, Seb murmured, "Ned, why call me over to see a shrimp?"

Ned sniggered, and sounded relieved, now that Seb had spoken. "Thought you wanted to see your little friend," he said.

"M-m—" Midget tried to break away, but the hypnotic smile seemed to grip him and sap his will to move. He hated this power Seb possessed, this power over others, but most of all over him—the power that could hold him with a look, and enter his mind, and make the dark jaws open to devour him.

"Friend?" Seb didn't take his eyes away, and his voice was soft and melodious, as though he were talking to the person he loved most in the world. "That's too big a word," he went on musically, "for such a very small person. You'll have to shorten it. Take the 'r' out of *friend* and what do you get?"

"*Fiend*," chuckled Ned. "Oh, very clever."

"Take the 'r' out of *brother* and what do you get?"

"*Bother*," said Ned and laughed out loud. "You're just showing off 'cause you won again. Where did you get all this fancy word stuff?"

But Seb didn't answer. His manner had changed suddenly, subtly, from the pretense of nodding sympathy to a stillness so complete that the unfailing smile now seemed chiseled into his face. The eyes didn't blink, didn't flicker, as they watched and waited.

"M-m—" Midget tried to look away, but the other will seemed to rivet his gaze. The smile enveloped him in an over-powering effulgence. He felt Ned shift slightly, and the thought came, that even Seb's best friend was secretly frightened of him. But that was no help now. He saw the eyes widen, until they seemed to become the whole face.

I know what you want. I know what you're waiting for. Well, you won't get it.

But already he felt the first tremor, fluttering through the muscles of his arms in its horribly familiar way. Within seconds, another twitched in his stomach, a third in his thighs. They had not shown outwardly; but he knew Seb had detected them. The smile deepened, and the soft, sympathetic voice lilted back.

"It's going to have a fit, Ned. One of its famous attacks. It's trying to hold it back, but it won't manage it. It never does, poor thing."

Another tremor broke out in his stomach, stronger than the first. The thigh muscles started to lock, then the arms, hands, toes. He felt his eyes bulge. Seb's face became a blur, but the smile lingered and was the last thing he saw before vision was snuffed out. Gulping for air, he fell back against the railings. Seb's hand caught him at the back of the neck, pretending to help him up, but all the time twisting his hair into a ball of pain.

The fit burst upon him like a flood.

When he came to, he saw only shadows. The shadow of Seb, the shadow of Ned, and other shadows standing around him like ghosts. The hand that had twisted his hair in secret now stroked it.

Another shadow bent down, and he heard Jenny's voice. "Is he going to be all right? He looks terrible."

"He'll be okay." Seb's voice exuded concern. "The worst's over now."

"He hasn't had one as bad as this before, has he?"

"One or two. They've been getting worse lately, since he started running off to look at that boat he wants. You know, I told you about it. Dad's explained to him often enough why he can't have a boat of his own—well, you can see for yourself why he can't. But he still keeps going to see it. The crazy thing is, the one he wants isn't even finished, and looks like it never will be. The builders stopped working on it weeks ago for some reason, and haven't gone back to it since."

Midget felt a flicker of energy in his body, but even his anger could not summon enough strength to hit or scratch or spit, or even snarl. Jenny said, "Poor little thing," and he felt her hand touch his face. He started to cry, not from pain, but from reasons he could not comprehend.

Seb picked him up.

"Come on. Let's get you home."

"Can I help carry him?" said Jenny.

"I'll do it. I feel bad enough as it is."

"But it's not your fault he had an attack."

"I know. But I still feel responsible."

They walked home in silence. And Midget bounced up and down in his brother's arms and went on crying.

During the evening his sight came back, and the cramps eased, and Dad decided not to call the doctor. Seb made a pot of tea and some scrambled eggs on toast, and they both encouraged him to eat and drink what he could. He didn't want anything, but Seb cut the pieces and fed him, and he didn't have the will to refuse. Afterward Dad carried him upstairs, put him to bed and kissed him, and went back down to watch the cricket highlights on television with Seb. An hour later they both came upstairs, and the lights went out.

Midget stared up at the dark screen of the ceiling, his body so weak he could barely move a hand to wipe the sweat from his face. He closed his eyes yet again, yearning for sleep, certain that at least tonight, after all that had happened, Seb would not come.

But Seb did come.

To taunt and torment, and remind him of his death.

three

"Last time we met," said the psychiatrist, "you mentioned that your son had gone off on his own, against your wishes, and had an attack." Midget saw the specialist glance his way for a moment like a kind of benign lizard; but the eyes quickly turned back to Dad. "And you added that you guessed where he was. What did you mean by that?"

Dad shrugged, and fingered one of the roses in the vase close by him. "He's got this thing about a boat down at Old Leigh. A sailing dinghy. Keeps running off to have a look at it."

"What kind of a boat? Don't get too technical." A suspicion of a smile appeared, but was soon gone. "Sailing's not my strong point."

"Well, this boat's not even finished. It's still sitting in the boatyard, abandoned. The builders have obviously got better things to do."

Midget thought of the hull lying on its own. Abandoned? Not abandoned. Not by me anyway. Whatever they say.

"But what kind of a boat was it meant to be?"

"It's just a local one-design class. This boatyard in Old

Leigh is the only place that builds 'em. Quite a clever design, really. They're single-handers, but they also go well with two. Only got one sail, but it's stepped right up in the bow. There's about twenty or so down at the club, and they race. Very competitive. Seb's got one."

The psychiatrist raised his eyebrows. "Does he win?"

"Usually." Dad played with the roses again. "There's no one to touch him down at the club."

The psychiatrist was silent for a moment, and Midget wondered what he was thinking. But the face was so inscrutable it was as though the features resented any movement away from blank immobility.

Dad mopped the sweat on his neck with a handkerchief. "The thing is, all three of us can sail. But the point about this boat is, he couldn't have it anyway, whether it's finished or not. Not a single-handed dinghy. In case he . . . you know . . ."

Midget frowned at him. In case I have an attack.

The psychiatrist leaned forward. "But would you allow your son to have a boat like that even if he didn't suffer from these attacks?"

"No," said Dad without hesitation and glanced at Midget apologetically. "You know the reason. We've been through this so many times. It's not that you can't sail. You can. I know that. But—" He seemed at a loss which of them to speak to, and finally turned back to the psychiatrist. "These boats, they're only small but they're very lively in a strong wind. They capsize easily, even with experienced people at the helm."

Midget felt the muscles around his mouth twitch. He knew what Dad was going to say next. There was hardly any point in listening. I can't have a boat because I might have an attack, and because I'm too small and puny to be able to keep a dinghy like that upright.

". . . a dinghy like that upright," concluded Dad.

Snap. Almost word for word. Except he didn't say puny.

The psychiatrist was looking over again.

Now you're wondering where I do most of my sailing. If I'm that keen.

"Your son seems so keen, though. Where does he do most of his sailing? With you, presumably."

I do most of my sailing in my head. I always have.

"I take him out in *Trade Wind* and give him the helm when I can. But he particularly likes Ray-Days."

"I beg your pardon?"

"Ray-Days." Dad took a moment before he seemed to realize that not everyone in the world knew about the tidal features of the Thames Estuary off Leigh-on-Sea. "It's really called the Ray Gut. But most people just call it the Ray." He used his hand to try and draw what he was describing. "It's a channel, see, about a mile offshore. Parallel to the land. Quite deep in the middle. It stays filled with water when the tide goes out."

"With mud banks on either side?"

"That's right. You get a big inshore mud bank that stretches about a mile out from the land. Then the Ray channel. And then on the seaward side of the Ray, another bank. The South Bank."

"How wide is the Ray?"

"Depends on the state of the tide. Couple of hundred yards usually. We go to the South Bank, obviously."

The psychiatrist's slight raise of an eyebrow was sufficient to query the obviousness of the idea.

Dad noticed and cleared his throat. "Most people can't get to the South Bank without a boat. That's why we go there. And it's better anyway."

"Don't people swim across the Ray, then?"

"Some do. You've got to be a strong enough swimmer to get across and back again before the South Bank gets covered by the flood tide."

"Oh, I see. The South Bank gets covered when the tide comes in. So you basically maroon yourselves on the South Bank?"

"Exactly. And like I say, if you haven't got a boat, you can only get there if you're a strong enough swimmer."

Midget saw the psychiatrist's eyes slant toward him.

I don't know what's in your mind. But I do know what you're not thinking about. I bet Dad doesn't.

True to form, Dad misread the glance. "My son wouldn't try it. He can't swim."

Well done, Dad. Add another one to the list of things I can't do.

The psychiatrist frowned. "I wasn't thinking that," he said slowly.

"Aren't we wandering off the point a bit? I thought we were supposed to be filling in more of my son's background?"

"We are," said the psychiatrist, and Midget wondered if that meant, we are supposed to be doing so, or we are already doing so. He had a feeling it was the second.

Then the psychiatrist spoke again.

"Did you realize that the moment you mentioned the Ray, your son stopped his nervous twitching?"

Dad shrugged. "I wouldn't read too much into that. And I do think we're getting off the point."

But the psychiatrist went on, in his quiet, smooth voice. "Tell me what you do on these Ray-Days."

Dad paused, seemingly for thought, but Midget knew it was to master his impatience; and he had a feeling the psychiatrist understood this as well as he did. Eventually his father went on.

"You choose a day when the tide's going out early in the morning, then you sail out to the Ray with the ebb, and when the tide's gone out, you're marooned in the channel for six hours or so until the tide comes in again in the afternoon. Then you sail home."

The psychiatrist took off his glasses and ran a finger over them. Midget noticed how white the hands were, how slender and well shaped they seemed, compared with Dad's, which were rough and chunky, or his own, with their warts and blemishes and chewed nails.

"And what do you do on these Ray-Days?" he repeated.

Again, Dad shrugged. "You meet friends out there. Either they sail out with you, or walk out from the shore. Lots of people go sometimes. It's good fun. You can play softball on the mud, walk, swim, things like that. Kids like to fight to be the last on the South Bank before the water covers it when the tide comes back in."

"That sounds dangerous."

"Not if you've got a boat or you can swim well enough. And you'd be pretty stupid to get yourself caught on the South Bank on a rising tide without having a boat or being a strong swimmer. You'd deserve to drown."

A bluebottle fly burst in through the open window, whirled back and crashed into the pane, seeking escape, then, just as quickly, was gone. Midget stared after it into the sky, and let the picture of the estuary float into his mind in the usual way, and with it the boat, as much a part of the scene as the waves themselves.

He heard the psychiatrist speak, and to his surprise, realized it was to him.

"So you like to do all these things, do you, young man? Play softball and so on?"

He shook his head violently, and looked to Dad for help.

Dad sighed. "All he ever wants to do is sail. It's the one passion he has. It's what drives him. That's the problem. It's made him obsessive about something he knows he'll never have."

Midget looked at him, then at the psychiatrist, and the two faces, one grim and sad, the other passive and unemotional, seemed equally remote. For a reason he did not understand, the clear water in the vase of roses seemed to turn red like the flowers themselves, and seep over him in a stream, as he imagined blood would flow from a deep wound. Then the stream widened and merged with the picture of the estuary spreading through his mind.

But the water remained red. And this time, he saw no boat.

On the train home he tried to put the boat back into his mind. But all he saw was an empty space. And the space seemed to grow larger until it engulfed not only him but the whole world.

In place of the boat, he thought about Mom. He still called her that, in his wordless inner speech to her, even though he had never known her. At home he pored secretly over the photographs in the family album, as he had done numberless times, when no one was looking. But the pictures only told him how she looked, not how she moved, or spoke, or laughed.

Or whether it really had been his fault.

Or whether she would have loved him.

He closed the album, and the image of redness came back, of the roses dripping blood, and with that picture came the taunts and accusations and threats of vengeance that Seb flung at him when he came during the night, and that crashed into his mind and lodged there, whimpering inside him. Not that the threats were new; Seb had always said he would kill him when the time was right. But it was only recently that he had promised it would be before the end of the summer holiday.

And Seb always did what he promised.

The stream of thoughts flowed bloodily on, as if to drown his mind, and with it the dream, and all else, except guilt.

four

Midget hung back, sweating already in the early morning sun, as Seb reached up and rang the doorbell. The usual vigorous barking erupted inside the house, followed by the sound of huge paws scraping the other side of the front door.

Midget stepped back another foot. He had already been thinking it might be possible to slip back through the gate while Seb was not looking. The pawing and panting inside made him even more anxious to escape. But Seb read his mind, and leaned quickly back.

"Don't get any ideas, Mad Midget," he murmured, his voice smooth and friendly, matching perfectly the engaging smile that beamed protectively down. "Don't try and slip away."

The eyes were warm and bright as the sun, the voice like a musical charm. Even now, with all he knew of Seb, and with his last words still so fresh, it was hard to believe in the icy hatred beneath the surface, as deep as his own, yet so much more subtle.

He heard footsteps inside the house, and half turned toward the gate. But the slight change in Seb's eyes was enough to draw him back. The melodious voice, which everyone loved when it told stories or jokes, or sang at Christmas, chimed softly close to his ear.

"And another thing, Mad Midget. I've seen the way you keep trying to get Jenny's attention. Just because she's sympathetic. Well, I don't like it. So it had better stop. I'll be watching you."

The smile widened and washed over him again.

He looked down and tried to bring the boat back into his mind. He knew Dad had insisted that Seb take him to Jenny's this morning to keep him from running down to the boatyard again.

The familiar argument started on the other side of the front door.

"Have you got him?"

"You get him! I've got my hands full!"

"You're closest!"

"I told you. I'm doing this, aren't I?"

"Well, I'm busy, too."

There was a derisive laugh. "Reading the paper!"

"Where's Jenny?"

"Where do you think?"

"All right. I'll go."

He heard the sound of the violin up in the back bedroom, strangely in contrast to the noises below, then footsteps in the hall, more loud barks, and a thud against the door, followed by a curse close by.

Seb laughed and rang the bell again. Slowly the mail slot squeaked open and two eyes peered out. Seb laughed again.

"Hello, Ben."

The eyes sparkled at once. "Oh, it's you. Come to see my daughter, I suppose. Hang on. Henry's plonked himself right against the door, and I can't move him."

"We'll go around the back."

"No, hang on." The mail slot snapped shut and there was a sound of scuffling and grunting on the other side, and a few more curses. Finally the door drew open about a foot, and Ben's bovine face appeared, beaming at Seb. "Seb," he said in his slow, drawling voice, "can you squeeze in over this mountain?"

The great dog lay sprawled across the entrance and clearly had no intention of moving. Seb stepped over easily, and Ben clapped him on the shoulder. "Well done, young man. Every day a new challenge." He touched Henry playfully with the side of his slipper. "Very little brain in there, see, Seb. Very little brain. That's the trouble with it."

Midget shifted on the step, and Ben seemed to see him for the first time.

"So you've come to join us, too, little fellah?" Ben's joviality was as unconvincing as ever. "Great. Jump in, if you can."

Midget hesitated. He hated big dogs, especially unpredictable ones like Henry.

"Don't be frightened," said Ben. "He's just a big baby really."

"Let me," said Seb, and before Midget could step back, he felt himself lifted high over the dog and put down in the hall.

Ben chuckled and gave him a wink. "What it is to have a caring older brother. Come and have some gingerbread." And without a backward glance, he put his arm around Seb's shoulders and led him through to the kitchen.

Alone by the front door, Midget tried to calm his thoughts and think what to do. He was sweating even more now, not from the heat but from where the big hands had gripped him, and kindled recollections, only too recent, of what they could do, what they preferred to do. In the kitchen, behind the door already closed to him, he heard Seb making Ben laugh, and Margie asking if he wanted gingerbread.

Probably they had thought he would follow automatically. Or maybe they hadn't thought anything. He knew he was an embarrassment, no matter how jocular Ben might appear, or how motherly Margie would be.

And she always calls me pet. I hate being called pet.

They don't want me. I'm not good-looking and charming. I don't come here every day, and chat them up, and have them eating out of my hand.

I'm not going out with their daughter.

I'm . . . I'm who I am.

I'm what I am.

He looked back at the front door, wedged half open against the body of the dog, now dozing noisily at his feet. Through the gap he could see the alleyway at the bottom of Woodfield Gardens leading down toward the estuary.

One big jump and I'm away.

The top of the cherry tree in their own front garden across the road swayed in the breeze. He gazed back toward the estuary, and as if to mock him, the picture of the boat floated into his mind, and out again. Then he heard a quiet voice behind him.

"Hello."

He turned and saw Jenny, with the violin under her arm. She was standing at the foot of the stairs, watching him with an expression he found hard to understand.

Either she feels sorry for me, or she's wondering how to get away from me as quickly as possible and join Seb. He felt a restlessness in his hands and thrust them into his pockets, certain she would want to move on to the kitchen. But she smiled suddenly, and said, "How are you?"

He dropped his eyes, wondering what to do, then looked up again, and saw she was still smiling, though it was a shy,

41

inward sort of smile. He forced his mouth into the shape of the word as best he could. "G-g-g—"

She let him stammer on for a few moments, before showing him she understood. "I'm glad you feel good. I've been worried about you since that last attack."

He tried to think of something friendly to do, and eventually pointed to the violin.

"How's it going?" she said, and he nodded. She snorted, not at him, but at the question she had phrased for him. "Don't ask. I call it the vile-in these days. That's the way I seem to play it at the moment." She frowned, as suddenly as she had smiled. "Why have you been left here all on your own?"

He glanced toward the kitchen, wishing he could tell her he'd rather stay here with her than go and join the others. Then she said, "Come on. I think Mom's made some ginger-bread."

He looked back through the front door, but this time she mistook his meaning. "Leave it open. We need some fresh air in the place with all this heat. And there's always the hope that Henry might wander off and get lost."

He followed her down the hall. And as he walked, he saw she was still frowning.

The kitchen door opened to the expected scene: Seb sitting on the high stool by the window, facing into the room. Ben and Margie on chairs drawn up on either side of him, both doubled up with laughter at something he had just said. Ben looked around at Jenny and wiped his eyes.

"Listen, love, you've got to stop Seb cracking these jokes. He'll finish us off. I'll have to take early retirement."

"Thought you'd already done that," said Seb, and Margie laughed.

Jenny still didn't smile.

"Don't you think you ought to welcome your other guest,

42

too? Instead of leaving him on his own by the door?"

Midget saw all eyes turn to him, and shuffled around wishing they would look away. Margie bustled to her feet at once.

"I didn't know you were here, pet. Ben never said anything. And your brother started telling us one of his stories, and—"

"Thought he'd gone up to have a chat with Jenny," said Ben. "Didn't know he was just standing there like a lemon. You should have come through, boy."

Midget flushed, not least at the suggestion that he could ever have a chat with anyone. Jenny placed the violin on the table. "Maybe he was waiting to be invited," she said quietly.

For a moment no one spoke, and Midget moved from one foot to the other, avoiding their eyes. He knew Seb was watching him intently. Margie dusted her hands and opened the cake box.

"Okay. Who wants some of this?"

"Me!" said Ben.

"Guests first. Seb?"

"Thanks." Seb took some gingerbread and calmly ate a piece, making appreciative noises as he did so, to Margie's obvious delight. Then he turned to Jenny. "How's the practicing going?"

Midget watched her, wishing the tension in her face would stay, yearning for her to answer Seb with the coldness she had shown to her father. But no one ever treated Seb that way. Not even Jenny. She shrugged. "Pretty bad."

"Sounded okay to me," said Ben.

"Well, you don't know anything about it."

"Charming," said Ben and rolled his eyes at Seb. "It's been like this ever since she started the latest piece. Old Man Brahms must be laughing in his grave."

Margie held out a plate. Midget took it, and gripped it hard so as not to drop it. He knew Seb was watching him again, in secret, and wondered how much longer he could bear to stay in the room. Sweat broke out over his face and neck. He thought of the open door, the road, the estuary. And again, the boat.

Damn the boat.

He tried to throw it out. But it was back in his mind and would not leave. And somehow it called him.

Jenny was offering him gingerbread, and smiling. He loved it when she smiled. She was so often serious and intense, and smiles made her less remote. He stared back, uneasy at her closeness.

Seb's voice slid into the confusion of his thoughts. "Great gingerbread. Try it."

The plate he had gripped too hard slipped from his fingers and shattered on the floor. He stepped back, knocking over a vase of flowers, which smashed, too.

"M-m—"

Jenny took his arm. "It's all right. It doesn't matter."

But he broke from her, and bolted into the hall. The dog looked up from the open front door and growled. Without a moment's hesitation, he leaped over the animal and raced away toward the boatyard.

But the boat was nowhere to be seen.

He stood outside the yard, gasping for breath. Looking at an empty space.

Suddenly the foreman came out and, to Midget's surprise, looked straight at him and smiled.

"You 'ere again! We'll 'ave to give you your own key!"

Midget stared back, wondering why the man had chosen to speak to him today, having never done so before.

The foreman took a gulp of tea from a huge mug.

"I know what you're looking for. Well, you're all right. The boat's still 'ere. Just been moved, that's all. Go in an' 'ave a look if you want."

Midget pushed past him eagerly, and savored his first-ever entry into the yard. All thoughts of Seb and the others dropped away as the atmosphere of the place enveloped him. He could smell wood, and what he thought was tar; he could see chains and spars and greasy blocks, and men rubbing down the hull of a motor launch at the top of the slipway. Someone deep in the yard was working a lathe. Another was hammering. Somewhere else, hidden behind one of the hulls, a man was singing, slightly out of tune.

The foreman came up and pointed to the far corner of the yard. "Over there."

Now he saw the dinghy, still propped up on the same old chocks, the bow facing toward him as it had done in its old place by the entrance. But today it was different.

The hull had been painted, a light, pleasing yellow, and the decking around the cockpit varnished. Suddenly the boat seemed almost ready to sail. The dream came back at once, and he thought of the mast stepped and the sail drawing, and the boat racing out from the shore.

The foreman's voice broke in again. "Won't your dad let you 'ave the boat? I just thought, you bein' so interested. Never seen nobody so interested in a boat before."

Midget looked up at him, and shook his head.

The foreman shrugged. "Well, if you can't 'ave it, you can't 'ave it."

At once a high, breathless voice broke in behind them.

"Can't? Can't? Don't know that word!"

Midget turned and saw an old man he had never noticed in the yard before. He seemed far too ancient to be working; yet he was wearing overalls, and held a paint can in one hand and a brush in the other. The cap on his head looked as

45

though he had put it there years ago and not taken it off since.

The foreman laughed. "This 'ere's Joseph, son. Joseph, the Miracle Man, that's what we call 'im. You'll soon find out why."

Midget looked up at the old face with growing interest.

"But 'e's off 'is rocker," said the foreman. "I'm warnin' you in advance."

"A miracle," spluttered the old man, his eyes darting restlessly at them. "That's what you need."

"Not now, Joseph. Give us a break."

"A miracle. That's the answer. Nothing's impossible."

"Nothing's impossible?" The foreman threw back his head. "That's crazy, even by your standards. Some things can't be done, an' that's final."

The old man turned abruptly and hurried over to the dinghy. "There you go again. Can't, can't. No wonder you never see no miracles." He started repainting the hull. "Ain't got time to talk. Got to get 'im ready for the Skipper."

The foreman chuckled, nudged Midget, and lowered his voice.

"That's Joseph's way o' talkin' about the sea. 'E always calls it the Skipper. Stupid old fool."

He took another swig of tea.

"'E's a bit of a cantankerous old man, but 'e won't 'urt you. Mind's gone, that's all."

The old man coughed suddenly and with such severity that Midget looked up at the foreman for explanation.

"'E ain't well. 'Is 'eart nearly give out a while back. 'E on'y come back from the 'ospital yesterday. That's why you never saw 'im when you first come sniffin' around."

Midget looked back at the old man, painting with unusual speed.

46

"Funny, though," said the foreman. "'E can build a boat like nobody can. An' 'e didn't want none of us touchin' this dinghy while 'e was away. Told me 'e'd be back to finish the job 'imself, no matter 'ow ill 'e was."

The foreman shook his head and lumbered off to the other side of the yard.

The old man coughed again, the same violent, retching cough, but did not interrupt his painting except to wipe his mouth with his sleeve. He seemed unaware of everything but the boat. Midget edged closer to the hull, checked that the varnish didn't look wet, then ran his finger along the decking.

"Stop that!"

The old man had been facing the other way and hadn't turned around, yet the voice snapped at once, as though Midget had touched him rather than the boat.

"Don't you touch 'im! You don't know 'im yet. An' 'e don't know you."

Midget stepped back, wondering how the old man could have seen him without turning around. Even now Old Joseph did not look his way or stop painting.

He wondered how to frame the question the old man had just put in his mind, and he eventually pointed at the boat.

"H-h-hi-him—?"

To his surprise the old man understood at once.

"Why 'im, not 'er for a boat?" He coughed again. "Boats are like people. Better'n people, really. Everybody reckons boats is a she. But there ain't no truth in that. They can be a 'e or a she. All depends."

Midget pointed at the hull. "W-w—?"

"This one? Told you, didn't I? This one's a 'e. No doubt about it."

"H-h—"

47

"'Ow do I know?" The old man dipped his brush again. "Just do."

It was strange the way the old man understood him so easily. An idea occurred to him, and he wandered around the stern and looked at the transom. Once more, the old man seemed to know what he was doing without turning to look.

"You won't find no name on 'im yet. 'E don't want me to tell nobody 'is name. Not till 'e sees the Skipper. You don't give nobody 'is name till 'e's properly baptized."

The old man fell silent again, and Midget began to sense an urgency in the brush strokes, and an unwillingness to tolerate further interruption. But there was one more question he knew he had to ask. One word the old man had said that would not go away. He wondered how his mouth would cope with the task of pronouncing it.

"M-m-mi—" he began, his body swaying with the effort. But the shape was starting to come. "Mi-mi-ra-c-cle."

He wiped the sweat from his face, hoping he wouldn't have to say it all over again.

Old Joseph looked hard at him for a moment, then suddenly pointed around the yard with his brush.

"There's so many miracles in this place alone as would stop you an' me walking through 'em. If on'y you could see 'em."

"Y-y—?"

"I see 'em all the time. 'Ave done for years." He pointed to the foreman on the slipway with a group of men. "See 'im? 'E wouldn't believe in no miracle if one come up and slapped 'im in the face. Same as the rest of 'em."

Midget looked around the yard, wondering what so many miracles looked like.

"Not that way!" said the old man testily. "You don't see 'em outside. Not first." He tapped himself on the head. "In 'ere. That's your own personal boatyard. That's where you build your miracle boats. You start with a picture. You got to make a picture. You got to see 'em real clear, every detail. An' you got to want 'em like you never want nothing else. An' you got to believe in 'em too. Total. No doubts."

"B-b—"

"Oh, I know." The old man held up a gnarled finger, splotched with yellow paint. "You're thinkin' miracles 'as got to be on the outside. Well, they is, eventually. But they start inside. You build 'em in your boatyard—" He tapped his head again. "You see 'em good, want 'em good, believe in 'em good." The ancient face seemed to light up. "Then you launch your miracle boats down the slipway an' they sail into your life."

"Dah!" The gruff voice broke in behind them. Midget turned and saw the foreman back again, his hairy forearms besmeared with grease. "What a load o' garbage. All that stuff about seein' things an' then they 'appen. I been seein' myself winnin' the lottery the last twenty years an' I ain't never got a dime. So that knocks that argument on the 'ead."

The old man looked at him balefully, then turned and spat. "That's 'cause you don't picture good enough. You don't believe good enough."

"I believe somethin' *when* I see it. Not the other way around."

"Well, I ain't never seen Australia but I don't doubt it's there, do I?" Old Joseph broke off, coughing.

The foreman's expression softened. "Go 'ome, Joseph. You ain't well enough to work. Finish the boat another day."

But the old man painted on, still coughing, and after a while, having apparently forgotten they were there, started to speak in a strange, rambling way, his mouth close to the hull, as though he and the boat were talking to each other. But Midget caught no words.

He felt a touch on the shoulder, and for a moment the icy fear came that it was Seb. But it was only the foreman beckoning him away.

They walked out into the main street of Old Leigh. The brightness seemed fierce after the shaded part of the yard where the dinghy lay.

The foreman winked. "Don't worry about 'im. Like I told you, 'e's a bit mad."

Midget wandered off down the cobblestone street to Bell Wharf.

Mad? Like me, Mad Midget?

The sun was high now, poised over him like a bright fist.

He walked a little way down the Cinder Path, then turned and looked back toward the boatyard, now hidden in the heart of Old Leigh.

Maybe mad people should stick together, he thought.

That afternoon he started drawing.

At first the picture came slowly, but after a while he managed to complete the outline and work on the details. Old Joseph's words came into his mind again and again, until he felt they were his own.

You see 'em good, want 'em good, believe in 'em good. Then you launch your miracle boats down the slipway an' they sail into your life.

He finished the picture and started another, exactly the same. It was just as well Seb was out with Jenny, and Dad busy at the shop. He worked hard at the second picture, and it turned out better than the first, though it still wasn't anywhere near right. He took another sheet and started a third.

In the evening Dad came back, and a few minutes later, Seb. He heard them talking and laughing in the kitchen, as Seb did the cooking.

When they called him for dinner, he walked down and took his place at the table and started to eat, and found he could see the pictures in his head, as clearly as on the pages he had left behind in his room. Neither Seb nor Dad spoke to him about his running away from Jenny's house.

After dinner he went back to his room and continued to draw until it was too dark to see by the natural light of the day. He looked out of the window at the darkening sky over the estuary, and the pinprick lights of Canvey Island and Kent far away, and for once the advent of night, which so often meant the advent of Seb, seemed less frightening. He switched on the lamp and drew some more, and tried to believe.

Now each picture was turning out better than the one before, his hand trembling less as his confidence grew. And the more he worked, the more he heard the gabbling, breathless voice in his mind.

He sharpened his pencil yet again and drew on and on, and when he heard them coming up the stairs, pushed the pictures under his bed, and switched off the lamp. Dad came in and kissed him on the forehead before going to his own room. Seb called a cheery good night from outside the door.

The lights went out, and he waited and wondered whether he would hear the soft footsteps and the slow twist of the doorknob tonight.

But he was to be spared this time. Maybe Seb was in a good mood. Or just tired. Or maybe this was a little miracle sent to encourage him. He waited another quarter of an hour to be sure, then switched on the lamp, pulled the papers out from under the bed, and continued drawing long into the night.

five

The psychiatrist took off his glasses. "I've been reading through the conclusions of the various doctors you have consulted, and also the comments of the teachers and special-needs staff who have worked with you over the years. And I'm starting to get some ideas that I'd like to explore with you today. They may or may not be correct. We'll have to see."

Midget sat snuffling in the armchair, trying to avoid both the unwinking gaze of the man and the midday sun slanting in through the window. The stickiness of the air and clamor of London traffic outside the window did not make their first session alone more palatable.

He glanced at the door and wondered what Dad was doing out in the waiting room. Probably reading the sailing magazine he'd bought at Fenchurch Street Station. Midget thought of the photo on the front cover. He liked sailing magazines, because of the pictures. It didn't matter that he couldn't read the words. He noticed that the vase of roses was gone.

"The first thing to say," the psychiatrist went on, "is that your nervous attacks should not make you feel in any way inferior to anyone else. Having said that, you need to recognize that there is a problem, and face it as honestly and courageously as you can."

On went the glasses. "So let's start by being honest and courageous. In particular, let's be honest. All right? You can tell me exactly what you think. It'll all be in complete confidence. And I'll tell you exactly what I think. Does that seem fair?"

It was clearly the moment to make some response. A smile or even a wink was out of the question, remembering last time. He decided on a nod.

"That's better!" The psychiatrist was trying to be chummy, but it didn't come naturally. "You're almost smiling!" The man's own smile was so brief it was hard to believe it had ever been there. The measured tone quickly returned to smooth away any residue of emotion.

"Now, let's consider those ideas I mentioned to you a moment ago. Remember, they may be wrong. We're just kicking around possibilities at this stage. Let's start with your nervous mannerisms." The psychiatrist looked down at some papers on his desk. "Your facial tics are still"—he glanced up, then back at the papers—"very much in evidence, as are the other twitches and so on that I noted at both our earlier meetings."

Midget shifted in the chair.

"The point is," he went on, "the shaking of the head and hands, the twisting of the body, the various movements of legs, feet, shoulders and so on, all of which you're doing now—it's all right, don't try to stop"—off came the glasses again—"all these things are highly conspicuous." He looked Midget straight in the eye. "They're very noticeable."

Midget shrugged. So I'm noticeable. What's new?

The psychiatrist picked up a slender letter opener from the desk and idly played with it, the sun glinting off the silver blade as it turned this way and that. "I want you to remember this word—*noticeable*," he said slowly.

Midget eyed the blade, unsure of where the words were leading.

The psychiatrist tapped the pointed end of the letter opener on the table, then, still holding it, stood up and went over to the window. "Let's explore this idea of being—noticeable, shall we?"

I'm not sure I like this.

"Because there are two angles I want you to consider. We could almost refer to them, in this particular context, as involuntary and voluntary. Let me help you understand what I mean by these terms."

Predictably the glasses went on, but, almost in the same movement, came off again, and this time were used to stroke the blade of the letter opener, as though to sharpen it. "The involuntary side is what we might call the part of you that you can't change. The thing you can do nothing about. The thing you can't control and therefore have to accept."

I'm beginning to see the way this is going. I like it less and less.

"Can you think what that might be, young man? What is the thing you cannot change and simply have to accept?"

He scowled down at the floor.

"It's your size, isn't it? Isn't that the thing you cannot change? And as yet, cannot accept?"

He twisted angrily in the confines of the chair. "S-s—"

"Please don't be upset," said the psychiatrist quickly. "I don't wish to cause you distress. I just want to help you see things—"

"S-s—"

"Please." The psychiatrist held out a hand in what was meant to be a calming gesture; but with the letter opener clasped in his fist, the effect was quite the opposite. He realized his mistake at once, smiled, and dropped the hand to his side. "The point is," he went on, "when someone is much smaller in stature than his peers, it is quite a common thing for him to try and make up for that smallness by being big in other ways."

Midget glared back and found himself wishing the man would prick his finger on the letter opener. For a moment, in his imagination, he could even hear the shout of pain, see the drops of blood on the carpet. But when the psychiatrist actually spoke, it was in the same even tone. And there was no blood.

"The fact that you feel so strongly about this—as I can see from your expression, and your, er, body language—shows how deeply you are concerned about your size. Which I can quite understand. Of course. Anyone would."

I don't like this. I don't like this at all.

The psychiatrist sat on the edge of the desk, still playing with the letter opener. "You don't need to frown at me. I'm not the enemy. Really. I'm here to help you. Make you see things."

But Midget looked down, and to his surprise found his mind once more drawing pictures of blood dropping before his eyes, darkening the carpet, as red as the water in the vase that day. The bustle of the traffic seemed to recede; the picture in his head grew more interesting, more desirable.

"Now these movements and mannerisms may—I say *may*—represent ways you have chosen, unconsciously, of making yourself, in the eyes of others, more—noticeable. In other words, bigger."

You are the enemy. You say you aren't. But you are.

The picture of blood on the carpet grew so strong he almost believed it was there.

"So, following this line of reasoning, the involuntary part of your problem, the bit you cannot do anything about, would be your size. The voluntary part would be how you choose to react to it." Midget saw the letter opener move, but he no longer knew if it were real or part of the picture in his mind.

You see 'em good, want 'em good, believe in 'em good. Then you launch your miracle boats down the slipway an' they sail into your life.

He could almost hear Old Joseph's voice, with its strange, breathless urgency, so different from the polished tone of the psychiatrist. "And these tics and twitches, and perhaps even the fits themselves, may—I repeat *may*—be things you started to do many years ago as an unconscious way of drawing attention to yourself. To make yourself more noticeable."

You see 'em good, want 'em good, believe in 'em good.

"I'm not saying that you don't wish to master these problems, or that they are easy to master. They have become habitual after so many years, and you are at present unable to control them. The treatment may or may not help. But what I am saying is that in the beginning you may have started doing these things as a way of getting yourself noticed, to make up for your lack of physical stature."

The glasses went on yet again. "And your need to be noticed may be linked to the yearning for this boat, in which you might be able to compete with and perhaps beat your brother, who, I understand, excels in the sport . . ."

The letter opener rose and hung poised like a fang.

"It might even amount to a desire on your part to hit back at what you see as an unfair world."

Midget closed his eyes and found the picture so vivid he could no longer doubt it.

"A desire for revenge," said the psychiatrist.

That's right. Revenge. On Seb, and on—

"Ah!"

He blinked his eyes open and saw the letter opener clatter against the desk, then fall to the carpet. The psychiatrist held up his hand. The index finger was dripping blood.

"Silly of me," he muttered. "I'm always playing with the thing. Keep forgetting it's got a sharp end." He glanced at Midget and laughed nervously.

Midget shrank back in his chair and watched through narrowed eyes. The picture in his head was gone. He realized it was no longer needed. It had become real.

He shivered.

"That's better." The psychiatrist was winding a handkerchief around the finger, his composure quickly restored. "I don't know what made me press the point to my finger in the first place. Still, at least I didn't drive it in too deep."

Midget looked down and saw a drop of blood on the carpet, the only one to have escaped the handkerchief. But it was a real drop, not just a picture. He tried to shake off the fear that was starting to grow within him.

The psychiatrist started talking again, urging him to remember what they had discussed, and not to take personally what had been said.

But Midget was already looking at a new picture.

A picture of what he had to do next.

He ran along the Cinder Path toward Bell Wharf, hoping the train delays on the way back from London hadn't made him late. Luckily there were fewer people around, now that it was the end of the afternoon, and he didn't have to dodge the bodies and stares of others at every step. He checked his watch again.

It'll be close. Very close.

The sun dipped unhurriedly over Two Tree Island.

He was just in time. The men were coming out of the boat-yard as he arrived. He watched and waited, then ran forward.

Old Joseph had come out, his strange, angular body bent forward as he shambled away down the road. The cap still rested on his head, somehow clinging on, but the old man coughed suddenly and it flew to the ground. He stared at it, coughed again, then stooped to pick it up. Midget rushed forward.

By the time he was there, Old Joseph had straightened up, and the cap was back in its place. But the watery eyes had turned and seen.

"What do you want?"

Midget shuffled to one side, trying to shape his mouth into the words he had been practicing all the way here. Suddenly the old man clutched him by the arm.

"Your boat ain't goin' nowhere. You got weeds around the keel."

The fingers were long and frail like withered rope. Yet they tightened.

"Weeds around the keel, that's what you got. You're sailin' in the wrong waters. Chasin' the wrong miracles." He grunted. "Most people got weeds like that."

Midget stared up at him, wishing he would let go of his arm and stop talking in a way that was hard to understand. But Old Joseph simply continued doing both these things.

"They don't check with the Skipper first, see? They go after the wrong miracles and get drowned. But that ain't the Skipper's fault."

The ancient face brightened. But it was a chilly brightness, like a candle in a skull.

The old man gripped his arm tighter still.

"Remember, some folk are real good at miracles. They can make 'em 'appen right away." The eyes darkened like wind over the sea. "But there's good miracles an' bad miracles. So make sure the Skipper's 'appy with what you want."

"W-w–?"

But Old Joseph merely nodded and said, "Make sure the Skipper's 'appy with what you want."

And he shuffled off, not looking back.

Midget watched him go, unsure whether his questions had been answered or not. And on the way home, and during the evening and the night, after Seb had left him, he found he still did not know.

But he had started wondering about the Skipper.

six

In the morning he took the papers down to the kitchen, found a cool spot in the corner, and sat on the floor, drawing. It felt good, if a little reckless, not to hide what he was doing anymore. But he told himself he had to learn about believing, and though he wasn't sure how to go about it, he felt certain that defiance in the face of Seb's inevitable reaction would at least give him confidence. As if to put him straight to the test, the door swung open.

Despite his good intentions, he could not stop himself reaching out to bundle the papers together. But Seb's foot came down on his hand, making him squeal with pain.

"What's this? Can't you think of anything better to do than draw crummy little pictures?" Seb kicked some of the papers with his other foot.

"M-m—"

"Don't mumble at me, Mad Midget. And stop wagging your head around like a dog. I'm not going to tear your pictures up yet. I'll have a drink first." He released Midget's hand. "Get me some orange juice."

Midget snarled up at him, yearning to resist, but aware of

the grim range of consequences if he did so. Seb's foot prodded him, as if to remind him of those consequences. He waited a moment longer, hoping Dad might come in; but even now he could hear his father sawing wood at the bottom of the garden. He struggled to his feet, shuffled to the fridge and pulled out the carton of orange juice.

"And don't spill it," said Seb, lounging back against the sink.

He poured, both hands shaking despite his efforts to control them, and put the glass on the table; then he started to fill one for himself.

"Stop that! The rest's reserved."

Midget clutched the carton to himself and whirled around to face his brother. He didn't know whether he wanted to throw it or drop it, or run with it. He only knew he had to do something. Something defiant, something to show his will, his hatred, his strength.

His belief.

Seb narrowed his eyes. "Put it down, Midget," he murmured, and stepped forward.

Midget scuttled behind the table, still clutching the carton, and dashed for the door. But Seb grabbed him easily. In an instant he felt the carton twisted from him, his back thrust against the wall. Then the large fingers closed over his throat.

To his relief he heard Dad's step outside the back door.

At once the arm pinning him back slid around his shoulders in a protective gesture. The fingers that yearned to strangle now ruffled his hair. The voice changed to meet the new situation.

"Dad, quick! He's going to have an attack!"

Dad came rushing in.

"Where is he? Where is he?"

"Easy, Dad, easy." Seb stood back, breathing hard. "I think . . . I think I might have stopped it."

"What did you do?"

Seb looked away modestly. "Don't know. Just kept stroking his hair. It's probably got nothing to do with it."

Midget slid back to his place in the corner and glowered up at them both. The admiration on Dad's face was almost as insulting as the innocence on Seb's.

"I'm sure it's got everything to do with it," said Dad and looked down at Midget. "You all right?"

Midget looked away in disgust.

"What's all that paper doing on the floor?"

Midget pushed one of the pictures toward him. "Dr-dr—"

"Drawings? You've never done any drawings before. Colored, too. Good boy. I'll have a look at them later." Dad stomped over to the sink and splashed his face with water. "I'll be glad when this darned drought's over."

The back gate clicked.

"That Jenny?" he said.

"Yup."

Dad stepped out of the door. "He's in the kitchen," he said gruffly, and made off down the garden.

Jenny came in, eyebrows raised. "What's up with your dad?"

Seb shrugged. "Nothing. Drought's getting to him, that's all. Don't worry about it. Want some orange juice?"

"Thanks."

Midget caught Seb's eye and saw him give a wink back, as though the two of them were special friends and shared some great secret. Jenny saw the wink, turned, and suddenly noticed him in the corner.

He looked down, trying not to stare back at her as he wanted to, hoping she wouldn't speak to him and make him feel awkward because he couldn't answer. But she came over and stood by him.

"Are these your pictures?"

"M-m—"

She bent down and he felt the long hair brush his head.

"Sorry," she said, pulling it back. "It's always getting in the way."

Holding it in one hand, she bent closer, and he saw she was frowning, as she studied the drawings. He felt sure they must look awful to someone as artistic as she was. But she smiled.

"They're very good. But why do you keep drawing the same boat?" She held up one of the sheets. "It's Seb's, isn't it? Or Ned's?"

Seb walked over and handed her a glass of orange juice.

"My boat's not yellow," he said. "Neither's Ned's. You know that."

She took a sip of juice. "But it's the same type, isn't it?"

"Same *class*, doll. It's called a class."

Midget saw her lips tighten at the word *doll*. It was rare for Seb to make such a blunder. He prayed earnestly for another.

"Same class, then," she said after a moment. "It is, isn't it?"

"Well, it's meant to be."

She studied the picture again. "I think it's good. Very clear. Lots of detail. But"—She looked across at him suddenly. "Why do you keep drawing a yellow boat? There aren't any yellow ones at the dinghy rack, are there?"

Seb took the sheet from her. "It's the boat down at the yard. The one he's been running away to look at."

Midget snatched the paper from him. "M-m—"

"It's okay," said Seb. "I won't hurt the picture. I think it's great. I told you that earlier."

"He's right," said Jenny. "They're all good. You could have a talent you didn't even know about."

Seb nudged her. "We're supposed to go sailing, remember?"

She glanced out of the window. "There's not much wind. We'll have to paddle, won't we?"

Seb grinned. "We'll have to take Midget along as galley slave to work the oars."

There it was. Blunder number two. Another little miracle. Midget felt a twinge of pleasure as the joke fell beautifully flat. Seb laughed, but it was no good. Jenny's smile was gone.

"I . . . I didn't know you called him that. That's not very nice."

Already Seb's smile was at work. "I was only joking. He knows that." Again the conspiratorial wink. "It's just a private joke we've got, him and me."

"S-s—" Midget hissed, and felt his mouth start to froth. Jenny watched him silently, and for a moment he thought she knew something of his pain.

Seb put his arm around her. "Come on. Let's go."

But she leaned down, touched the picture with her hand, and said, "I hope you get your boat one day. I really do."

After they had gone, he sat back against the wall, listening for a while to the sound of sawing in the garden. Then he bundled the pictures into a carrier bag, stole out to the road, and headed for the estuary.

They were finished.

Just as the pictures were finished, so, too, was the boat.

He gazed at the yellow sides and varnished deck, gleaming now that the men had moved the boat into the sunlight. The mast was stepped, the rudder shipped, centerboard, buoyancy bags, toe straps all in place. Sail, battens, and sheet lay in the cockpit ready for use.

A FOR SALE sign stood on the foredeck.

He tried to ignore it, and remember what he had drawn,

what he had worked so hard to believe. That a dream on paper could become a miracle in wood. A miracle for him. He clutched the bag, and looked around for the man he had come to see. The man who knew about miracles. The Miracle Man.

Then he heard the foreman's voice behind him. It was kind and low. And grave.

"'E's gone, little man, 'e's gone."

It paused as a train rumbled past. Then it spoke again.

"An' 'e ain't comin' back no more."

He wandered, dazed, toward the seafood shacks, the way the foreman had told him to go. Usually he liked to walk this way, especially if the shacks were open and they were selling prawns and whelks and jellied eels. But now everything was different.

Everything was going wrong.

Just when he'd started to feel a slender faith in the future, it was slipping away like the ebb tide now flowing down the Creek toward the Ray Gut and the open sea.

So much for the Skipper.

He stared out over the shelly beach at the ribs of the old wreck sticking up like slimy teeth through the surface of the shallows. Once he had made up stories around that wreck.

Now it was the story of his life.

The only boat he'd ever have.

Out in the sparkling waters of the Ray, the garden of sails seemed to mock him. He plodded on toward Leigh Station.

Miracles? Maybe the old man's wrong. Maybe there aren't any miracles. Maybe there never were any miracles.

He frowned. There won't be any now.

He reached the station, and looked left to where the road

curved around the bank. And there, floating alongside the jerry, was the oyster boat.

It seemed only right that a crazy old man like Joseph should have a crazy old home like this. He looked over the ancient hulk, wondering why he had never realized before that this outlandish craft, which he had seen so many times on his walks, was the dwelling place of a strange and unforgettable person. He stared at the tattered rigging, the boom and gaff lying across the deck, the long bowsprit pointing out to the estuary it would never cross again, and he thought, the boat's dying too.

Just like Old Joseph.

He climbed on board and walked over to the hatchway, folding and refolding the note the foreman had given him to pass on. Through the opening all looked dark below, so dark that at first he saw no features at all of the inside of the cabin. He leaned forward and listened.

No voice came. No sound of movement. Then he heard breathing.

Slow breathing. Rasping, gasping, painful breathing. He hesitated, then, as briskly as he could, clambered below.

Even with the hatch open, the cabin seemed murky, and there was an eeriness, which the solitary oil lamp did nothing to dispel. Coils of rope and bundles of sails formed dark, hillocky obstacles as he made his way further into the cabin. He felt a deep silence, but no peace.

Old Joseph lay in a bunk, staring up at the underside of the deck. By the bunk was a half-eaten piece of bread, and a mug knocked on its side. The old man didn't move.

Midget fiddled with the note, and cautiously stepped forward. His foot knocked the mug and sent it rattling into the bow, where it disappeared in the darkness. He heard the quiver of a voice.

"Don't ask the Skipper . . . for bad miracles . . ."

He turned and looked on a face as still as a sculpture. But there was a trickle of saliva around the lips. He took his handkerchief and wiped it away.

"Always make sure the Skipper's 'appy," said the voice tiredly. "'E don't like it otherwise."

Midget stared down, trying not to believe what was happening. But the voice was growing weaker and he knew it would not be long.

"If you want a bad miracle . . . an' you see it good . . . an' you believe in it good—then you'll get it. Only somethin' else comes with it."

The old man took a long, slow breath.

"Evil comes with it."

The glazed eyes turned toward him for the first and last time.

"An' evil comes before death. Like a wraith."

Midget stepped back. He didn't know what the last word meant, but there was something frightening about the way Old Joseph said it.

Still the eyes held him, and for a curious moment he felt they were like a dark mirror, and he was looking deep into himself. Then, as though the old man had no more to say, they slowly turned and stared back up at the deck.

Midget thrust the note forward, with its thick, untidy writing. "Just to remind 'im I'm 'ere, case 'e needs anythin'," the foreman had said over the stub of the pencil. "An' to send you back with any message."

But Old Joseph didn't read it. The eyes rolled upward and seemed to rest under his forehead.

Midget watched, unable still to accept that the mystery of death was unfolding before him. Suddenly the old man shuddered.

"Get the boss," he muttered.

Midget moved closer to the figure lying in the bunk.

I won't see you again. I won't—

Without knowing why, he reached out and touched an eyelid with his finger. And the old man murmured, "Nobody don't see no more. They're all . . . blind."

Panic overtook him. He dropped his bag of pictures, scrambled out of the cabin and onto the jetty, and raced back to the yard, weeping as he ran.

He didn't need to try and speak. The foreman took one look at his face and hurried off toward the old boat. Midget bolted along the Cinder Path.

But there was no escape in flight. His thoughts ran as fast as he did, and when he finally stopped at Jocelyn's Beach, gulping for air, the pain was with him still. Sunbathers and passersby stared. An elderly man asked him if he was all right.

He broke away and stumbled along Chalkwell Beach, past the bowling greens and the shelter, dimly aware of the road stretching ahead toward Southend Pier. A car honked at him, faces jeering at the windows. Two skinheads jostled him as they slouched past. A man in a wheelchair knocked him to one side and rolled on without a word. Children, taller than he was, ran up and capered about him, chanting. He clapped his hands over his ears but the thoughts chased him still, with a chant of their own.

The Miracle Man is dead.

He pushed the children away and ran up Chalkwell Avenue, anything to avoid people, anything to keep running. But he knew neither was possible forever.

Two hours later, he found himself outside the house. He

didn't know where he'd been. He hobbled to the door and put the key in the lock.

The Miracle Man is dead.

He turned the key and entered the house, and saw Seb standing before him.

And soon I'll be dead, too.

seven

But death was not to come that night. And in the morning, when he awoke, he heard a strange voice downstairs.

Strange because he knew it, yet his mind would not supply a face. Suddenly the door opened and Seb appeared.

"You've got a visitor." The pseudosmile beamed at him. "Put your bathrobe on and come down."

Midget glared back, but the smile only deepened. Dad's voice called up, "Is he coming?"

"He's on his way!" shouted Seb.

Midget walked over, pulled on his bathrobe, and made his way down the stairs. In the hallway he saw his father and the owner of the unknown voice.

It was the foreman from the yard.

Dad was trying to look relaxed, but a frown kept appearing as he spoke. "Mr. Kemp here, he runs the boatyard down at Old Leigh. As you . . . obviously know." He turned to the foreman. "I'm sorry he's been spending so much time hanging around there. I hope he hasn't gotten in the way."

"Oh, 'e ain't been a nuisance. "'E's a super boy."

"Yes, well—" Dad shifted uneasily and looked quickly back

at Midget. "Anyway, the point is, Mr. Kemp found out our address at the sailing club because he's got some news for you."

The picture of the boat floated into his mind.

The foreman cleared his throat. "That's right. You see, boy, you made yourself a friend down at the yard. An' I don't mean just me."

"This old boatbuilder," said Dad.

"Crazy loon!" said the foreman. "Mad as they come."

Midget looked from one face to the other, but all he could see was the picture in his mind.

"Funny I never saw him around," said Dad. "If he was as distinctive as you say."

The foreman burst out laughing. "Oh, you couldn't miss 'im if you saw 'im. But 'e didn't go nowhere much. Just to 'is boat, or to work. Didn't drink or 'ave no social life or nothin'."

The picture was so clear he could almost smell the paint.

"Anyway," said Dad, "this old man died yesterday. And it appears–there was some kind of will."

"That's right." The foreman held up a scrap of paper and unfolded it with fingers clearly more accustomed to handling rope and chain. "'E made me put yesterday's date, an' write down what 'e wanted, an' get another guy in from the street to be the other witness, an' 'e managed to sign it before 'e died."

He squinted at the paper for a moment, then in a slow, solemn voice began to read.

"'This is my last will and testament, me bein' o' sound mind.'" Here he snorted. "'I leave my boat *Estuary Maid* to Ernie Kemp at Old Leigh boatyard, an' I leave all my money to 'im an' all.'" He looked up. "It was stuffed in a bag under 'is bunk. 'E didn't 'ave no bank account."

"Was there a lot?" said Dad.

"Not much. But enough to carry out the last part of the will."

Seb walked slowly across the room and put a hand on Midget's shoulder.

"And what might that be?" he said quietly.

The foreman looked at the paper again. "'I leave all my money to 'im an' all, provided 'e makes sure that yellow dinghy . . .'"

But Midget heard no more. He no longer needed to. Even the touch of Seb's hand could not disturb him now. He closed his eyes, and as the others talked, saw the picture in his mind break free.

He leaned his shoulder on the foredeck and tipped the boat on the launching trolley, and for the first time, felt with a thrill the weight of the hull under him. He stroked the foredeck; the wood seemed cool in the entrance to the boatyard, despite the fierceness of the sun. He ran a finger along the cutting edge of the bow and dreamed of it slicing through the water.

"Aren't you going to take the cover off?" said Jenny.

He turned and saw them all watching him: Dad, Seb, Ben, Margie, and Jenny, a range of expressions on their faces. And only Jenny's seemed to show pleasure.

Dad stepped forward. "We'll do that at the rack. No point in fiddling around now. Let's get things moving."

The foreman lumbered over. "I put all the gear inside the cockpit."

"Very kind of you," said Dad.

"An' I left the cover on just to show the little guy how it's laced up."

"Good. We'll sort it out."

"'Spect you will," said the foreman, unperturbed by Dad's impatience. "You got yourself a place on the dinghy rack, then? That was a bit o' luck. Thought they was pushed for space down there."

"They are," said Seb. "But someone just vacated a space."

The foreman looked down at Midget. "One miracle after another, eh? Maybe that crazy old fool 'ad somethin'."

"Okay!" said Dad. "Let's go!"

Suddenly everyone was bustling.

Midget looked this way and that, wishing they would all disappear and let him pull the boat along on his own, find the rack space on his own, take the cover off, hoist the sail, launch the boat, on his own. This moment was special, and he wanted to savor it alone.

But they were all too busy to take the slightest notice of him. Dad had taken the launching trolley and was swinging the bow toward the street. Seb was at the other side of the hull, helping to pull. Ben had lifted the mast onto his shoulder and was waiting for the others to move before he turned with it. Margie had picked up the life jacket; Jenny, the burgee. They moved off, leaving him standing with nothing to do.

They think I'm helpless. They think I can't do anything.

They think I'll never manage the boat on my own.

He clenched his fists and glared after them. Then he realized the foreman was still with him.

"Good thing you got so many people to 'elp." The man winked. "Just in case, like."

Midget looked away.

In case what? In case I have one of my fits? In case I capsize the boat because I'm not strong enough to hold it up in a breeze?

He stamped off after the others. They were already close to

Bell Wharf, and even Jenny hadn't noticed he was not with them. They reached the start of the Cinder Path and pressed on toward the rack. Now he saw Jenny turn and, seeing him so far behind, slow down for him to catch up to her.

"How do you feel?" she said.

He noticed she had shortened the length of her stride, so that he could keep up.

"You must be amazed at getting the boat you spent all that time drawing."

He looked at her and tried to smile.

"Do you think you'll be able to handle the dinghy on your own?"

At least she'd come out with it. Not like the others. Bustling around, pretending their doubts weren't there. Even if the faces did betray them.

He looked down, wondering if she knew of the doubts in his own mind.

Then she said, "You'll manage the boat. I know you will. I believe in you."

He wanted to answer. If only to thank her.

"My . . . violin teacher," she said shyly, "he keeps saying you've got to believe in yourself and let the instrument be like another limb. It's got to become part of you until–until, in the end, it becomes all of you. Does that sound stupid?"

It didn't sound stupid. It sounded like something Old Joseph might have said, only in a different way.

"N-n-n–"

She lowered her voice further, as though afraid of her own words.

"Well, maybe a boat's a kind of instrument, too. Once you know how it works, how you . . . play it . . ." She hesitated. "Then it can also be like another limb. It can also become–all of you."

She fell silent and seemed reluctant to speak again. He saw the others waiting at the rack, their faces like those of mourners at a funeral.

He pondered her words and thought, maybe today is a funeral. A funeral for my old body.

Maybe I've got a new body now.

A better one.

At the rack, he found the boat propped up at the top of the slipway. Dad and Ben were down at the water's edge, having a cigarette. Seb had wandered off to check his own boat. Margie came up with the life jacket.

"Here you are, pet. You'd best put that on, seeing as you can't swim. Seb won't want to dive in and fish you out if you capsize."

"Mother!" said Jenny.

"I only said 'if.'"

He took the life jacket and walked to the edge of the rack. Easterly breeze. Force three to four, gusting to five, the shipping forecast said. He closed his eyes tight.

I mustn't capsize. I must show them I can hold the boat up. For Old Joseph's sake. And Jenny's.

And mine.

He heard footsteps on the planking and saw Dad and Ben on their way up the slip, chuckling over some private joke. Seb joined them, and all three started to unlace the cover. He stepped forward.

"It's all right," said Dad. "We'll rig the boat this time. It'll be quicker. You just watch so you know how it's done."

I know how it's done. And you know I do.

His body started to twitch.

But no one noticed. Dad and Ben rolled back the cover as far as the stern decking, and bent over the cockpit to feed the sail along the boom. Margie and Jenny slid the battens in. Seb attached the burgee and stepped the mast.

Midget watched, and raged.

"She's a lovely boat," said Jenny. "What are you going to call her?"

Old Joseph's words came back, and to his surprise, his own rushed out.

"H-h-he!"

The others turned and stared.

"H-h-he!"

He gasped for breath, feeling the silence and stillness of them all, and their awful scrutiny.

"Can't be a he," said Seb. "All boats are a she. You know that."

"It's got a name already," said Jenny. "I can see one of the letters on the transom."

Ben walked around to the stern. "You're right. The old boy must have given the boat a name just before he kicked the bucket."

"Ben!" said Margie.

"Sorry, love."

The others crowded around, and Ben started to unlace the last part of the cover. As Midget watched, Old Joseph's words came back once more.

'E don't want me to tell nobody 'is name. Not till 'e sees the Skipper. You don't give nobody 'is name till 'e's properly baptized.

He looked at the boat and thought, you've come to be baptized now.

And to baptize me.

And to become my new body.

To become me.

Maybe being me won't hurt so much now.

"It's a funny name for a boat," said Margie.

He walked toward them, hearing only the pat of his canvas

shoes on the planks of the rack, now that the others had stopped speaking. They moved aside for him, and he knelt down and stared at the jumble of letters on the transom, expecting to understand nothing.

For a reason he could not explain, the letters made no resistance to him, and formed at once into the words.

For a reason he could not explain, he read the name aloud, without a single stammer.

"*The Miracle Man.*"

So you're still alive, Miracle Man. And you've come back to me.

Suddenly none of the things that had bothered him earlier mattered anymore. He let the others blab on about the funny name of the boat; he let Dad and Seb fiddle with the sail, and the rudder and tiller, and check over the buoyancy bags and toe straps, and do all the things he knew he could do himself.

They can rig you this time. I'll do it next time. It doesn't matter.

It didn't even matter that he heard Ben whisper to Margie, "That boy'll never handle the boat on his own," or Seb to Dad, "Don't worry. I'll pull him out when he capsizes."

Jenny said the boat was a nicer color than Seb's, and that was more than enough to compensate.

Seb ran over to get *Scorpion* rigged, while Dad and Ben backed *The Miracle Man* down the slip, floated the hull free, and gave the trolley to Margie to pull back up the slip. Dad hoisted the sail. It shivered in the breeze, as though eager to work.

Midget hurriedly pulled on the life jacket and fumbled with the lacing.

"Let me," said Jenny. She reached out and fed the lacing up through the eyelet holes. He trembled slightly under the light pressure of her hands. She tightened the lacing at the top, and tied it with a knot. "Don't forget," she said quietly. "I believe in you."

He climbed in and sat amidships for a moment, to let the rocking of the boat settle. Above his head the sail tugged the boom back and forth as the wind caught one side, then the other. He fingered the boom vang, the mainsheet and tiller, and the centerboard, waiting for him to slide it down into the water.

Dad began the inevitable lecture.

"Now listen, don't go out too far. Hang around near the rack until Seb can catch up with you."

Ben sniffed the air. "Getting a bit gusty."

Dad nodded. "Be careful. Ben's right. And it'll be stronger further out. So stay inshore this time. Okay?"

A stronger gust shook the sail, and the hull shuddered. He realized he was shuddering, too.

Miracle Man, don't let me capsize.

The bows were swinging away from the slip, as wind and tide nudged the hull out. He dropped the rudder blade, lowered the centerboard, and took his place to port.

"She's ready to sail," said Dad.

"H-h—"

"He's ready to sail. Sorry, forgot."

"Good luck," said Jenny.

"Good sailing," said Ben.

"I think the boat looks very pretty," said Margie.

Four pairs of hands grasped the hull and edged it around to face the sea.

Dad was still fussing. "Don't forget, the thing to watch out for in squally weather—"

But Midget had had enough. Before Dad could finish, he drew the helm toward him and pulled in the sheet. The timbers of the boat shook, the sail clapped and filled.

On a ripple of foam, *The Miracle Man* raced away from the shore.

Ben, Margie, and Jenny cheered, but Dad was silent. Midget glanced back and saw Seb wheeling *Scorpion* down the slip.

At that moment the first squall struck.

The starboard gunwale plunged under water, the sail brushing the surface. He scrambled up the windward side, hooked his feet under the toe straps, and leaned out as far as he could go.

Don't capsize, Miracle Man. Please.

The water sluiced beneath him, faster than he had expected. And the hull was still lifting.

I've got to show them. I've got to hold the boat up.

He strained further over the edge, determined not to cheat by letting out the sail to spill the wind. Still the port side rose.

Let the boat become part of you.

All of you.

Believe.

A wave crashed against the foredeck and doused him with spray. He gritted his teeth and inched himself further out. Gradually the windward side lowered.

He gave a whoop of triumph.

Water ran up his back and he slid inboard, feeling the gust weaken. The sail flickered along the luff, and he pulled it in until it was trim. *The Miracle Man* surged forward, cutting an effortless path through the inshore seas.

Scorpion was reaching out toward him, Seb balancing the boat far more easily with his extra weight. Midget saw an arm beckoning him inshore.

I won't. I won't.

His brother beckoned again, more impatiently. Midget thought of the others watching from the slip, and reluctantly headed on.

The boats crossed paths, each driving fast through the low waves. Seb motioned him to follow.

The exhilaration was gone. He wanted to ignore the command but knew there would be trouble tonight. Exactly how much might depend on what he did now.

He jibed *The Miracle Man* around and followed *Scorpion*. A short distance in front, Seb turned to look back.

"So you finally got yourself a boat, Mad Midget. Well, don't expect me to come and help you when you have an attack."

At the very mention of the word, he felt a tremor in his muscles, as he knew Seb wanted. He tensed them hard, but the tremor remained, and tried to spread. A large wave rolled over the foredeck and washed away down the side.

"You shouldn't be sailing at all," Seb went on. "It's not safe giving a boat to a loony."

The muscles twitched with greater force, controlling him one by one.

"The moment you have an attack out here, you'll capsize. And then you'll probably drown. You can't swim. And the life jacket won't do you any good if you black out and get caught with the hull on top of you."

The tremors deepened as Seb's picture dug further into his mind. He looked down at his body and gritted his teeth, trying to command it to be still. Suddenly he heard Seb shout.

"Watch out! What do you think you're doing?"

He blinked up and saw *The Miracle Man* only a yard from *Scorpion*'s stern, driving in as though to ram.

He thrust the helm down and hauled his wind, just in time. *The Miracle Man* skewed away to port.

It took him a moment to realize what had happened. And what it meant.

He had caught up with Seb.

"Idiot!" said Seb, but he took no notice. Instead he luffed further, keeping well clear so as not to steal the wind from *Scorpion*'s sail; then he eased off the sheet and bore away on a parallel course.

Now the difference in speed was obvious. Smoothly, steadily he pulled away from Seb. *The Miracle Man* heeled further, and he leaned out with all his strength, just able to keep the hull upright. And as he strained his body and mind to the task, it suddenly came to him that the tremors had gone, and for the first time in his life, an attack had been repulsed.

The Miracle Man raced on, away from the land, away from Seb, water showering into the cockpit as he met the larger offshore waves. He flicked open the self-bailers and sailed on, gazing ahead at the line of fishing boats in the Ray, and the tankers far beyond in the Main Channel.

And *The Miracle Man* stormed toward them like a beast uncaged.

But miracles had their price.

When the shadow came that night, he knew it would not be for words alone.

Pain was the levy of his existence. Just by being what he was. He wondered how much he would have to pay for today's success.

"Keep out of my way when I'm racing," the voice hissed, as the hands twisted his ears so hard he felt he would bite through the gag. "And I don't want to see *you* in the race tomorrow."

The pain in his ears was enough to persuade him against such folly. But he knew Seb would want more than that.

When it was over, he lay back on his bed, too exhausted to sleep. And he found himself talking to the Miracle Man again, in the silent speech of his mind that already seemed so natural.

No racing for us, Miracle Man. No racing for us.

eight

The Miracle Man nosed off from the slip and away from the rack to follow the flotilla of boats skimming toward the starting line. About a hundred yards ahead, Ned was leading in *Raider,* broadreaching on starboard tack toward the pole that marked the outer end of the line.

Seb was already there, waiting.

Midget watched *Scorpion's* dark hull flash as his brother rounded the pole and surged inshore towards the sea wall. *The Miracle Man* broached slightly, demanding his attention. He sniffed the air and checked the flag.

Strange how the wind had gone around to a westerly since yesterday. But it was just as gusty.

The ten-minute gun sounded from the race hut, and he set the stop watch. *The Miracle Man* yawed with the wind on the quarter, and he moved inboard a few inches to steady the roll. Glances came at him from the other dinghies, mainly of curiosity, but some of annoyance as the others realized how fast *The Miracle Man* was.

Seb raced back toward the outer end of the line. Ned luffed under his stern and followed him out, the two of them leaning close, talking. One by one the other boats reached the line and turned along it, either inshore or out in the wake of Seb and Ned. Midget kept on course for the outer pole, trying to work out what to do if he reached it at the same time as *Scorpion* and *Raider*.

To his relief they both turned and raced back toward the middle of the line, where a few of the others were gathered, some jockeying for position, others spilling the wind from their sails as they sat out the minutes before the start. He looked up at the boards on the race hut and studied the numbers of the buoys he had to sail around. The course was as expected.

A beat up to Old Leigh to split up the pack, a reach out to the Ray, a broadreach in to Chalkwell Beach, and back through the starting line to complete one lap. Three laps in all.

He patted the hull. Miracle Man, let my first race be good.

The outer pole, slimy with weeds, slipped by to starboard. He ran on toward Jocelyn's Beach, leaving the other boats behind, and tried to work out his tactics for the start.

It was obvious. Hit the center of the line bang on the gun, starboard tack, heading seaward. Further out would pick up more flood tide, which would be helpful, but he'd be too far downwind of the mark and the other boats. If he started inshore, he'd have the weather gauge, but the land would blanket the wind from him, and the flood would be weaker.

Center of the line then. The obvious place to start. He noticed the pack already gathering there.

Miracle Man, that's where we've got to go. Right?

As if in reply, a picture flashed into his mind, as clear as on a television screen, of the pack pouring over the center of the line. And *The Miracle Man* crossing from inshore.

He pounded the side of the boat.

That's a stupid picture. No idiot's going to start that far inshore.

But the images still danced in his mind. He glowered up at the sail.

I'll do the thinking, Miracle Man. You just get on with the sailing.

Still the picture hung before him, an inner world drawn across the outer world, more powerful, more vivid somehow than the gold of the beach, the smell of the sea, the warmth of the breeze.

The five-minute gun sounded.

He jibed the boat away from the beach, the picture still forcing itself at him, though curiously broken up by the view of Southend Pier in the distance. He luffed further, aiming for the oil refinery on the Kent coast, then went about and headed for the starting line.

By now it was crowded with multicolored sails, eerily interwoven with the picture of the same sails bulging in his mind. He saw the real *Scorpion* in the thick of the pack, fighting like the rest for clear wind and the best place to cross. But in the inner picture, he saw Seb leading the way across the center of the line, the pack snapping at his heels.

And again *The Miracle Man* crossing from inshore.

He pounded the boat again. You're wasting your time, Miracle Man. I'm not starting from inshore. It's the wrong place.

He rushed in toward the seawall, the hull heaving under him like a surfboard on a bed of foam. Passersby on the Cinder Path stopped to watch. He strained his body out, determined to keep the boat on an even keel.

The seawall rose before him, water licking up it like a giant tongue. He shot around onto starboard tack toward the center of the line.

Suddenly the pack looked different.

Where before it had moved, now it seemed still. Like a wall, blocking him from the line.

He rushed in, searching for an opening.

None appeared. His hands twitched, his mouth grew dry. One moment the boats seemed like a vast, single hull, monstrously engulfing the line. The next they were an endless mosaic of flashing colors. *The Miracle Man* surged in.

Suddenly a gap opened to starboard. He plunged through it into a thicket of sails.

At once boats closed in like teeth. *Scorpion* flashed past the bow and disappeared in the pack. Others followed, this way, that way, stealing his wind as they passed. He glanced at the stopwatch.

A minute to go.

Ahead the path to the line was blocked by more boats than he could count. The original picture forced itself back into his mind. And this time he knew he had to obey.

He thrust the helm down and tried to find a way back to the shore.

Now the wall he had broken to get in closed upon him as the outer columns of the pack began to sweep toward the line.

"Starboard!"

"Starboard!"

Two boats aimed straight for him on starboard tack, both helmsmen quick to remind him of their right of way. He altered course and steered between them.

"Starboard!" A third boat appeared on a collision course, the helmsman glaring around the luff of his sail.

He bore away, missing by inches. More boats appeared.

"Starboard!"

"Starboard!"

"Starboard!"

He weaved around them, hardly knowing how he dodged each one. Then suddenly he was alone, racing back toward the shore.

The starting gun boomed out from the race hut.

He heard the whir of blocks and the flutter of sails behind him. Over his shoulder he saw the pack swarm across the line. He forced the helm down again.

The Miracle Man spun onto starboard tack, and tore after them. He snorted.

Well, you got your way, Miracle Man. And a fat lot of good it's done us.

The pack was to leeward at least thirty yards in front, with clearer wind and more of the flood to push them up toward Two Tree Island and the first mark off Old Leigh. Seb was in the lead, Ned a boat's length behind, the others clustered astern like an armada.

I should never have listened to you, Miracle Man.

The bow drove into a trough and threw back a shower of spray at him.

It's no good you being playful. You should be trying to make amends. Like finding me a decent picture this time.

But the only picture he saw was of the boats ahead. There was only one way he could imagine getting past them. And that was impossible.

The old man's words snapped inside his head.

Nothing's impossible. Nothing's impossible.

He looked hesitantly at the boats and tried to picture the first thing he needed. A wind shift to force them away from Two Tree Island.

You got to see 'em real clear. You got to believe in 'em.

The sail crinkled along the luff. He bore away until it refilled. It crinkled again.

You got to believe in 'em.

He shuddered slightly. Ahead of him the pack had changed

direction, heading now for Canvey Point, unable to stay on the original course. Just as he had pictured. It had to be a coincidence.

He drew out from the shelter of the land and for the first time, *The Miracle Man* felt the true force of the wind. The lee side dipped, water swilled in, and he leaned out, his thighs aching with the strain. For the umpteenth time he cursed his smallness.

But the boat stayed upright, and the stragglers were drawing closer. He looked back at the picture in his mind, and thought of the second thing he needed.

This won't work, Miracle Man. It can't.

Again the words barked at him.

Can't? Can't? Don't know that word!

More spray flew back from the bow. He wiped his face and told himself firmly that if the first part had worked out all right, so would the rest.

And already the tiller was fretting in his hand, urging the bows back on the old course. The wind was veering, just as he had pictured, bringing the bows around again, past Canvey Point, past the entrance to Two Tree Island, in line with the first mark itself. Hardly daring to see if the rest of the picture was true, he peeped under the sail.

The others were well out of position, down to leeward and driving seaward, still untouched by the wind shift that had pushed him into the lead. And he was the only one who could lay the mark without tacking.

Because we started so far inshore.

He looked down at the boat. How did you know?

The Miracle Man powered on toward Two Tree Island, slicing through the seas or skimming over them, as the mood took. He shivered suddenly.

Why me, Miracle Man? Why can I do these things? Why can't everybody?

Foam burst over the foredeck, and sizzled back into the sea.

Some folk are real good at miracles. They can make 'em 'appen right away.

The shore slipped by to starboard as he tore toward the yellow buoy. Astern he saw Seb luff as the wind shift finally reached the pack. But none of them would be able to lay the mark in one tack. Some had already gone about, hoping to claw back to windward of the buoy. But they were well behind now.

The Miracle Man threw back more spray, like a horse tossing its mane. Midget gave a yelp and leaned out.

Another picture came, of *The Miracle Man* hurtling on and on to win, a picture now so real, so believable, it seemed to beg him to accept it, shape it, control it.

He didn't look back again. Until he had won.

The psychiatrist smiled.

"The twitching of your face and hands is noticeably diminished. And your manner seems somehow . . . less aggressive."

Midget looked up at him, but his mind was still on the race earlier that day. And this new feeling of strength.

"You look much more relaxed. That's good. It will help with the treatment."

He thought of *The Miracle Man* plunging over the line to victory. And the faces of the others afterward.

"Are you ready?"

He would have to face Seb later. That he knew. But the darkness was not here yet.

"Let's make a start. It will take a while to get you ready."

He noted, with a mixed feeling of guilt and amusement, a bandage on the psychiatrist's finger, and wondered whether they would find themselves fighting today.

But the psychiatrist seemed anxious to be friendly. "Okay, young man, I promise this won't hurt."

He felt a moist touch on his scalp.

"Keep still. These are just wires I'm attaching to your head."

He felt the first wire pressed against his temple, and held for a while until it stuck.

He leaned back and studied the white screen in front of him, with its curious pattern of squares in the middle. Looking around, he noticed a little booth in the back corner of the room, with what appeared to be an instrument panel.

"Please keep still," said the psychiatrist again. "I'll tell you what everything's for in a moment."

He half closed his eyes. At least this room was cool, and there weren't any flies buzzing around. He thought of Dad in the stuffy office next door.

"Biofeedback," said the psychiatrist, "is a method of feeding you information about yourself, so that through that information, you can learn to control yourself. I can't guarantee it will do anything to alleviate your particular difficulties. But it's an avenue we're going to try."

Midget felt another pad pressed to his head.

"These wires tune into your brain waves and give us vital information about what's going on inside your head."

The psychiatrist straightened for a moment to survey the wires he had attached, then leaned forward to moisten another spot.

"Now, what do we want to tune into these brain waves for? Well, quite simply, you have several different kinds of brain waves running through you. And they have names. Alpha waves, beta waves, theta waves, delta waves." He pressed on the next wire. "Alpha waves are the ones we're interested in. They may or may not help with these . . . attacks. But they can probably help you relax."

He straightened again. "What biofeedback can teach you to do is produce alpha waves at will. In a continuous flow. Okay, let's go."

He walked behind to the booth and flicked on a switch. Midget saw the screen in front of him light up.

"Now then. What do you see?"

He twisted around in the chair as he tried to force out the words. "R-r-r—"

"Good! Red. The squares are red. What about the screen?"

"W-w-w—"

"Take your time."

"W-whi-whi—"

"That's it. It's white. Red squares on a white screen. Now watch the red squares and tell me what happens to them."

"D-d-d—"

"Take your time. What's happening to the red squares?"

"D-dar-d-dar—"

"Well done. They're getting darker. Now what?"

"D-dar-d-dar—"

"Right. Even darker. Now what?"

He struggled to shape his mouth to the new sounds. "B-b-br-bri—"

"Good! They're getting brighter again. And if you just watch them a moment longer—you see?—now they're brighter than when we started. There, that's as bright as they'll go."

The psychiatrist switched off the machine and came back from the booth. "Now then, I want you to think of the red lights as signals. I can control them, as you just saw. But that was just to show you what they do. Once we start, I won't be controlling them. You will."

Midget looked at him doubtfully.

"When you're producing alpha waves continuously, those red lights will get brighter. When you're not, they'll get darker. It's as simple as that. All right?"

Midget gripped the chair.

"No. Relax. That's the first thing. Treat it like a game." He walked back to the booth and switched on the lights again. "Now, I'm not going to tell you how to do it," he called out. "There isn't really a technique. It appears to be an instinctive thing. Most people just find it comes gradually. Later on, if you find it very difficult, I'll give you some suggestions. But today, I just want you to experiment for yourself and see what happens."

Midget breathed in hard.

Relax. That's what he said. Treat it like a game.

"Ready?"

He nodded.

"Now, I'm going to switch off my part here, but the lights will stay on, and your brain will be controlling them. See if you can make the lights go brighter. And don't be discouraged if they go darker. Most people don't manage it the first time."

Midget frowned. This is stupid. How can I make them go brighter if you won't tell me what to do?

He stared at the lights. At least they were soothing to look at. Rather like the roses that day in the consulting room. He closed his eyes again.

I don't see the point of all this.

"Good!" The psychiatrist's voice rang out. "Well done!"

He looked up in amazement and saw the lights gleaming before him.

"Y-y–"

"I haven't done anything. You're in control."

He stared at the screen, wondering what he had done.

"See if you can make them go brighter still?"

He remembered the picture he had drawn that morning, during the race, and gazed at the lights, thinking how beautiful they would be if they were brighter.

Within seconds, they were at full brightness.

The psychiatrist cleared his throat. "Astonishing. It's as though you've been doing this all your life. See if you can make the lights go darker."

That was easy. He just looked at the lights and thought of the darkness of the night.

"Incredible," said the psychiatrist. "I've never seen anyone master the thing just like that. It's—"

The psychiatrist fell silent, and Midget inwardly grinned. Success in biofeedback was almost as enjoyable as success in racing.

"Let's make things harder. See if you can control the lights when I shout out the instructions quickly. Ready?"

There was just time to nod.

"Make them brighter!"

Easy.

"Darker!"

Easy.

"Brighter! Darker! Darker still! Brighter again!"

Easy. Nothing to this.

"Now I'm going to try and distract you. While you're controlling the lights, I'll deliberately suggest other thoughts. See if you can keep the lights on full brightness."

No problem.

The red light beamed at him reassuringly.

"It would be nice to be sailing down the Ray, wouldn't it?" broke in the psychiatrist. "Don't you think that would be nice?"

Ignore it. It's meant to distract me.

The lights stayed bright.

"What would your father say, if he could see you now?

93

Would he be proud of you? Or would he think this is a waste of time?"

You won't put me off that way.

"What would your brother say? I bet he'd be impressed."

He wouldn't be impressed. He'd sneer. He'd . . .

He felt his muscles twitch, and saw the light flicker. After a while he calmed himself and steadied the light. For what seemed a long time, there were no words from the booth.

"What would your mother say, if she were alive?"

A wave of cramps ran through his body. He doubled up with pain. The red light darkened at once.

Through a blur, he saw the psychiatrist leaning over him.

"It's all right, it's all right. I was only testing you. I know you think I was cruel. But I have to find things out."

"S-s—"

"I won't say any more things like that today. I promise."

"S-s—"

"You sit quiet for a few minutes while I take the wires off. Then you can go through to my office while I talk to your father."

Midget scowled and burrowed into his thoughts.

Later, alone in the office, he listened through the half-open door to the psychiatrist's voice in the next room.

"Very, very unusual. He could have abilities we don't realize, or he doesn't realize himself. People with limitations in one area can be highly developed in others."

The door closed before he could hear Dad's reply.

As he wandered with Dad up the hill from Chalkwell Station, he looked over the mud banks and tried to visualize Mom's face again. At first it was difficult as the thoughts of what lay in store for him during the night were starting to work on his mind. But after a while even these surrendered to the haze of his reverie, and the face came, and he almost felt that he knew her, that she was there with him, and in another moment, he would be able to speak without stammering and ask her the things he had always wanted to ask, and she would answer him. Then he realized something was wrong. Something outside his mind.

Walking toward him across the inshore bank was a figure.

It seemed eerily familiar, though the face was in shadow. It walked without hesitation, balancing neither left nor right, and only when it drew closer to the shore did he recognize who it was.

But Seb's out with Jenny. They're not coming back until this evening. He can't be here.

He turned to Dad and gripped his arm. Dad stopped and looked down at him. "What's up? You all right?"

He looked back at the mud bank and started to point.

But the figure was gone.

"I know," said Dad. "Nice view. Takes some beating, eh?"

Midget still stared over the mud, searching for places where the figure might have hidden. But he saw none.

"Come on," said Dad. "I'm getting hungry."

They walked on up the hill. But Midget still gazed over the estuary, wondering where the figure had gone. Or whether it had been there in the first place.

The figure was real enough when nighttime came.

"Loony's luck. Getting those wind shifts."

He won't kill me here. Not here. Not yet.

"Can't understand why you disobeyed my instructions. Going racing, I mean. Doesn't make sense, does it?"

Not here. Not yet.

"So tell me why you did it. Unless you feel so guilty you've got nothing to say?"

I've got plenty to say. Plenty.

But he could only gibber.

95

The voice tutted. "Champing your mouth again. And froth-ing. I've told you a hundred times not to dribble."

The pillow slammed over his face, snuffing out the breath. He gasped for air, blackness crowding on him. Suddenly it was released.

"There now, that's got baby clean. Though it nearly choked him, didn't it?"

The eyes moved closer; the fist nudged his windpipe.

"But it's not quite time for baby to die. It will be in a day or so. First he's got to pay for what he did."

The face was now so close he could feel the mouth against his ear.

"Even if you hadn't killed her, she'd have hated you any-way."

He knew an attack was coming, and that he wouldn't stop it. He tried to call on the Miracle Man, but all he could think of was death. Seb's presence blocked out all other thought. His body shook. He tried to find a picture that would help him, but all he saw was a misshapen insect, wriggling in the mouth of some huge, all-powerful beast, so vast that to over-come it, or escape it, was unthinkable.

His head started to roll. Cramps rippled through his mus-cles. He seized up, moaning, and fell off the bed. One of his hands shot into his mouth, and he found himself biting the fingers. He pulled the hand away, but instantly it returned, as though to mock his will. His eyes spiraled, scattering dots of light. For a second he thought of the moonlit waters of the Ray, shimmering like a specter's face. Then the black mouth opened and swallowed him whole.

nine

In the morning he thought of murder.

Not Mom's so-called murder, or his own. This was a murder he had never dared consider. Until now.

It's him or me, Miracle Man.

And we haven't got much time.

From his bedroom window he could see Dad in the garden, bent over the watering can, his shirt off already in the growing heat. He made his way down the stairs, listened at the kitchen door, then, hearing nothing, pushed it open.

"What are you staring at, Midget?" Seb lounged at the sink, peeling potatoes.

He kept his eyes on Seb's face and edged toward the back door, keeping the table between them. Seb watched in disgust, then turned back to the sink.

"So, did you have a nice time in London yesterday? I missed you terribly. It spoiled my whole afternoon."

This is going to take planning. Lots of planning and lots of pictures.

"The nice thing about spuds," said Seb, "is you can get rid

of all the dirt and garbage just by peeling the skin. Shame people aren't like that."

Lots of planning and lots of pictures. And lots of believing.

Seb finished one potato with methodical calmness, and reached for another. Midget watched, trying to think of something he could do to pierce that smooth assurance.

"I haven't decided where I'm going to kill you," said Seb casually. "Or how. But I may use some kind of blade." He held up the potato peeler suddenly, and chuckled. "Don't think I'll try this, though."

At once the picture flashed into his mind. The psychiatrist, the letter opener, blood. He closed his eyes tight, blocking out all disbelief.

"No. It's not nearly sharp enough for my purposes."

But it is for mine.

"Damn!"

He opened his eyes and saw Seb shaking his hand. Blood dripped into the water from a large cut.

The peeler lay in the sink.

"Damn!" said Seb again and whirled around. "Wherever you are, there's trouble."

He held the injured hand under the faucet and reached with the other to turn it on.

But Midget knew what would happen. He had already drawn it in his mind.

No water came from the faucet.

He moved back to the corner of the room, enjoying the confusion on Seb's face as he turned the faucet on full without success. Dad's face appeared at the window.

"Something funny's going on. Outside faucet's not working. Can't fill up the watering can."

"This one's not working either."

"I'll check no one's messing around with the mains in the

street. Ben's having some plumbing done sometime this week. It might be him."

Midget quietly watched the picture, reveling in the feeling of power. He saw Seb put his finger over the end of the dry faucet and rub it slightly to clean off the dirt.

It was too good a chance to miss. He looked into the picture and changed it again.

Water shot from the faucet, on full, and spurted up into Seb's face from the pressure of his finger. He leaped back, swearing, and turned the faucet down to half. Out in the garden Midget heard the watering can overflow.

Seb held his hand under the faucet, and the water turned red as it gushed over the cut. Dad's face appeared at the window again.

"Is it working?"

"You might have given me some warning. I just drenched myself with water."

"I didn't do anything. I heard it come on before I got to the mains. There must have been a blockage somewhere."

Dad tramped back down toward the bottom of the garden.

Midget watched his brother rinse his hand under the faucet, and closed his eyes, reliving the memory of that first picture.

"Damn!"

Again he heard the shout, and this time it was louder than before. He opened his eyes with alarm and saw blood flowing more thickly than ever from Seb's hand.

Dad came running up to the window. "What's wrong?"

"I just cut myself on the potato peeler."

"Deep?"

"Deep enough. But—" Seb looked down.

"But what?"

Seb frowned. "I cut myself once, and I was just feeling the

99

blade to see how it could have gone in so deep and . . . and I cut myself again. In exactly the same place."

"Well, you're an idiot. Put a bandage on and come and give me a hand in the garden. I need some muscle."

Dad disappeared, and Seb hunted in the drawer for a bandage.

Midget pressed himself against the wall, the feeling of pleasure draining from him, and fear taking its place. He looked into his mind and saw an animal with its own will, its own power, its own desires. Seb came toward him.

"I don't want to see you racing today, Midget."

And the hand swung down and cuffed him in the face.

He waited till Seb had closed the back door behind him, then wandered over to the window and looked out, wondering now whether the garden were real or just another picture in his mind.

He saw Seb appear around the side of the house and walk down the path. And as he watched, it seemed to him that the tall body grew fuzzy and indistinct, like the figure of a ghost.

The estuary lay like a sheet of glass. After the fluky winds he had conjured for yesterday's race, there was now barely enough breeze to carry the boats over the flood to the starting line.

He knew today's picture was his biggest challenge yet. It seemed so impossible that he wondered why he believed so completely in it. But his mind had seized the idea, as a ravenous wolf its prey, and now he was impatient to start.

He looked at the course-direction boards. The first leg, a beat toward the pier, now that the wind, what there was of it, had veered around since yesterday. No doubt the others would regard that as further evidence of its unpredictability. He smiled inwardly. Then it was out toward Canvey Point, back in to Bell Wharf, and around the course again.

He watched the picture quietly. No one would be expecting much action in this calm; probably half of them were wondering whether they would have enough breeze to struggle across the line. He let the picture unfold further in his mind.

The sun rose higher. He slid across the thwart, trying to find a spot shaded by the sail, but this only upset the trim of the boat, and he moved back amidships. The outer pole crept nearer. Boats ghosted along the starting line, others ponderously heading out in the hope of more wind. He saw Seb cutting toward him.

"Don't say I didn't warn you, Midget," he muttered as the boats passed.

The five-minute gun broke the silence of the waterfront. He eased the mainsheet, just enough to stop the bows crossing the starting line. The flood tide held him in check, and he took a bearing on the land to make sure he wasn't slipping back.

We're ready, Miracle Man. And the picture's ready, too.

Scorpion approached again, this time with *Raider* close by. He stiffened, waiting for the jeers, but all that came was a cheery hail from Seb.

"Not much wind today! Going to be a crawl!"

He hadn't expected Seb's public voice; then he heard the ripple of other boats nearby and understood. *Scorpion* and *Raider* luffed either side of him.

"Yup," said Seb. "Going to be a real crawl."

"Sure is," said Ned from the other side.

He heard the other boats again and looked to see which ones they were. *Moth, Tango, Long John.* He'd seen them often enough. All fliers, especially *Long John.*

But you're fast too, Miracle Man. And we've got the picture to help us.

"Bit of a dilemma," said Seb. "Do we start inshore and get

101

out of the tide, or stick around here and hope for a bit more wind? You're staying here, obviously. Think I'll do the same."

"Me, too," chimed Ned.

"Not that I can see us picking up any more wind than anybody else. But after yesterday's fluke—"

"Good pun," said Ned.

"After yesterday's fluke, I reckon I'll just stick with you in case you get lucky again."

"Maybe he's a mascot," said Ned. "He's the right size."

Midget glanced along the line again. The pack was well spread out, several boats clustered inshore, a small group shaping into position around the middle, and the rest of them out here. Seb and Ned had moved a few feet away. *Tango* and *Long John* were to port, *Moth* to starboard, hoping to squeeze between Ned and the outer pole.

The picture bulged in his mind, ever larger, ever more real. He saw the outer things, too: sails, flags, bright hulls; Seb coiling rope, Ned spitting. But the inner world was far stronger.

It was time.

He inched his way to the windward side of the boat, making the hull tip.

"What are you doing?" called Seb.

"Even *you* don't need weight up in this calm," said Ned.

He ignored them and continued to ease himself out. The boom swung toward him as his weight unsettled the balance of the boat.

Ned sniggered. "Not enough wind to dust a mirror and he's hanging out to windward like there's a gale blowing!"

Laughter came from the boats around him. Seb called across to them.

"We'd better rustle up a breeze for him. We don't want him capsizing before the race has even started."

He began whistling, and one by one the others joined in,

until "Land of Hope and Glory" sounded in ragged unison across the water, punctuated by bouts of laughter.

Midget tensed and looked for the picture again, and, for a moment of horror, saw that it had left his mind. Then he realized it was no longer needed there. And he knew where he would find it.

Up beyond the line the water was darkening into a vast ebony claw. As he watched, it thickened and seemed to stretch inky talons toward the boats, as though to pluck them from the surface and drag them under. Then the talons merged, the claw widened, and he saw the cat's-paw of the gale he had pictured all along.

Unaware, watching only him, the others clowned around the boats, some still whistling. He looked inshore at the other dinghies, but everyone seemed relaxed. No one was expecting any wind, so no one was looking for it.

The darkness raced toward them, gorging the water in its path.

"Not doing much good, this whistling," said Ned.

The starting gun went off, but there was so little wind now that none of the boats could even cross the line. He hooked his feet under the toe straps and moved further over the side. *The Miracle Man* started to roll toward him. The laughter stopped.

"What the hell are you doing?" said Seb.

Midget saw the water blacken around them.

"Can't you see there's no wind?"

At that moment the squall struck.

Even though he had summoned the gale, made ready for it, he was unprepared for its power. The hull reared and threw him down the cockpit, the lee side plunging with him. He thrust out a foot for something to climb on.

It went straight into the water. Somehow he grasped the thwart before he slipped over the side. But the sail still

103

dipped, rolling the hull with it. Water splashed into the cockpit.

His knee thudded against the gunwale. He braced himself against it, hauled himself up, and threw his weight over the windward side.

But still the hull roared, the sail pressing against the boiling surface of the water. He snatched the tiller and tried to bring the bows into the wind. The boat didn't respond and only heeled further.

The centerboard broke the surface, and he crawled astride the hull for the capsize drill.

That's not how I saw it, Miracle Man.

His thoughts seemed to shriek louder than the wind.

What have you done with my picture?

Suddenly the gust released him. The sail sucked free from the water; the hull slumped to an even keel. He scrambled into the cockpit, dug his feet under the toe straps, and pulled in the sail.

The Miracle Man thundered forward.

The speed was too frantic to give him time for fear. He was riding a wild beast whose only wish was to throw him off. He clutched the tiller and mainsheet, and screwed his eyes against the spray as *The Miracle Man* drove into the deepening waves. Water swilled about the cockpit, but he didn't dare lean in to open the self-bailers in case his weight tipped the boat again. He took a swift glance around.

The fleet was in chaos.

At least half the boats were capsized, and one had a broken mast, the sail drooping in the water like a limp cloth. Another was tangled in the mooring chains of a cruiser. The rescue dory scurried out from the shore.

But the best helms were still left. *Tango* and *Long John* surged after him a boat's length astern. *Raider* was a few yards behind them but had the advantage of the weather gauge, and was overhauling fast. *Moth* was close on Ned's quarter, battling with the dirty wind from *Raider's* sail.

He looked for Seb and to his surprise saw him heading seaward, his body pressed forward to help *Scorpion* punch through the waves.

A buffet of spray on his face brought his attention back to *The Miracle Man*. He threw everything from his mind except the need to keep the hull upright. The crash of the other boats seemed louder, but he forced himself not to look back. Under the boom he saw dinghies approaching from inshore, but they would pass astern. He kept his eyes on the luff of the sail as *The Miracle Man* pounded toward the seawall.

With a shiver of sails the inshore boats roared closer. He heard shouts of "Starboard!" from *Moth* and *Raider,* and the others altered course. As *The Miracle Man* raced toward the shore, he looked over his shoulder, trying to choose the best moment to tack.

Moth went about in a swirl of foam, followed at once by *Raider. Tango* and *Long John* tacked with them, and all four drove out toward the open sea.

He held on as long as he dared, wanting as much of the windward advantage as he could get on the next tack. The seawall was almost upon him. Figures strolled along the Cinder Path, some stopping to watch the boats, but most were uninterested in the battle he was fighting. Close by, he saw ropes from the running moorings, swathed in weeds. He rammed the helm down.

The Miracle Man spun around, almost too quickly for him, but he threw himself out the other side just in time. The hull lifted, and the boat rushed away from the shore. He looked anxiously for the others and saw them safely buried to leeward.

We'll do it, Miracle Man. If we keep on course, we'll be first around the mark.

The yellow buoy bobbed temptingly, just a few hundred yards off to port.

Two more tacks, Miracle Man. A couple of shorties.

Suddenly he remembered Seb.

He cursed himself, amazed that he could forget even for a moment his biggest threat. He stared out toward the Ray and saw *Scorpion* still racing seaward.

He's going for the buoy in one big tack. What do we do, Miracle Man? What do we do?

Keep on, came the thought. Keep on as you are.

He tried to concentrate on the sailing but found himself watching the dark shape cutting through the water out there with ominous speed, waiting for the moment when it would turn.

Suddenly it changed. Like the twist of a knife, it slid into a new form as *Scorpion* went about and raced inshore for the buoy.

He's on course, Miracle Man. And he's on starboard tack. He'll have right of way. Unless we get there first.

He drove the helm down, and the boat charged back toward the shore.

Keep it short, Miracle Man. Keep it short.

The beach seemed to rush toward him, as though it were moving, too. He checked over his shoulder for the buoy.

Ready about, Miracle Man.

Down went the helm again, and this time when he came around, he saw the mark dead ahead. And with it, *Scorpion*, bearing down from the seaward side. Now it was no longer a dark shape he saw, but the blue of the hull, the bulging whiteness of the sail, even the spray as *Scorpion* plunged and reared toward the buoy. And Seb's face, fiercely intent.

He mustn't get ahead of me, Miracle Man. Not for a single moment.

The wind gusted and he threw his weight out. And as he did so, a new picture slipped into his mind.

There was hardly time to think of it, with the buoy fifty yards away, and both boats on a collision course. But in the seconds he had, he seized the picture and let it possess him.

"Starboard!" Seb's hail rang out, as expected.

But he no longer cared about *Scorpion's* right of way. Not with the new picture. To his amazement, he heard himself hail back, his voice clear and loud, with hardly a stutter.

"Bull!"

"You little—"

But Seb had no time to finish. The squall hit them at that moment, just as Midget had pictured. Both boats heeled, but Midget had been ready with the sheet eased to spill the wind. From *Scorpion* he heard a crash.

The buoy loomed before him, then was gone. He bore away at once and raced for the next mark. There was no need to look around for Seb.

But he did so all the same.

As he stared back at *Scorpion's* capsized hull, he felt another moment of unease at the strange things that were happening to him. And he looked down at the hull, vibrating beneath him.

Tell me who you are, he said. Tell me where your power comes from.

And where you come from.

He glanced back again and saw *Scorpion's* mast tug itself free from the water as Seb pressed his weight on the centerboard and climbed back into the cockpit.

You're called *The Miracle Man,* he said. But who is the Miracle Man?

The others were at the mark now, squabbling for space. But Seb was around first.

Is it you? Or is it Old Joseph?

The wind gusted again, and the boat started to plane over the crests.

Or is it me?

He pushed the thoughts from his mind and focused on the next mark. But more pictures came, like sketches for him to complete, and he shaped them, and played with them, and watched them happen. And as he raced on to victory, he almost drove away the thought of what awaited him that night.

With the darkness, the old order returned.

He lay on his bed, too frightened to take off his daytime clothes, or even his shoes.

It'll be torture tonight. And then—

The door opened and the hands locked into his throat. He kicked upward but hit only air.

"Why did you kill her?" Seb breathed. "What right did you have to take the life of someone so beautiful?"

He kicked, and missed again.

"An eye for an eye and a tooth for a tooth. That's what the Bible says. Retribution. You must admit, that's fair."

He squirmed under the tightening pressure around his neck.

"That's what punishment's all about. Pain for pain. A life for a life."

The hands squeezed even tighter.

"Thought we'd go for a little walk tonight, Midget. Well, I'll be doing the walking. You can relax in this nice comfortable sack."

It's tonight. He's going to do it tonight.

"I know how you love Leigh Creek. Trouble is, it's very secluded on the marshes. You've got to be careful not to fall in the water. Especially if you can't swim. And suffer from fits."

He writhed around on the bed, but the hands held him like a vice.

"Now, we don't want to wake Dad. So I'll have to knock you out before we go. Sorry about that." Seb leaned forward. "But pain first. Seeing as you disobeyed me again today."

Midget flung his arm out and felt it brush the hard metal base of the bedside lamp. He closed his hand gratefully around it and brought it down with all his strength on Seb's head.

Seb gave a shout of anger and jumped up, brushing the lamp aside so that it smashed against the wall.

"You little–" he said, and reached forward.

There was a knock at the door.

"What's going on in there?"

At once Seb ran over. "Dad! Quick! He's having another attack."

Dad burst in and switched the light on, and his foot kicked the lamp lying on the floor.

"What the hell's going on?"

Already Seb had become the perfect, anxious brother.

"Thank God you're here. I heard this noise and came in to see what was going on. He was writhing around on the bed. I went over to help him–see if I could do any good–"

Midget scampered to the side of the room and glared up at them.

"But what happened to this lamp?" said Dad.

Seb held up his hands. "It's not his fault, Dad. He can't help it."

"You're keeping something from me. What is it?"

"Leave it, Dad. Really. He didn't know what he was doing."

"I know you're trying to stick up for him. That's fine. But I want to know what happened."

Midget saw Seb look over with an apologetic air, then, as though seeking the most diplomatic way out of a difficult situation, beckon Dad out of the room.

He wrestled to keep his body still, but it was as untamable as his mind. In a moment he knew he would either double up or black out. In desperation he searched for another picture to help him. But his thoughts ran too fast, his anger too deep.

Outside the door he could hear Seb's voice, calm, persuasive, believable. He knew where the finger of blame would point. The pressure in his body and mind mounted.

They came back in. Dad cleared his throat and looked down at him.

"Now look, we can't have you doing things like this. Not when Seb's trying to—"

But Midget burst past them, raced down the stairs and out through the front door.

He ran blind, knowing no direction, heedless of himself, of others, of anything. Gardens, walls, streets cascaded in a helter-skelter of images.

He drove his body until he cried from a stitch, then forced himself on further.

I hate you, body.

I hate you, horrible, midgety body.

At last he saw where he was. Somehow he had blundered up to the top of Somerville Gardens. Panting hard, he turned and ran down the hill toward the estuary.

I hate you, body. I hate you so much.

The headlights swung around the corner at the bottom and raced up toward him, the glare bouncing as the car sped over the bumps.

Panther's eyes. Demon's eyes.

He ran down toward them.

Be my friend, he said, and leaped from the curb.

In the split second of flight, poised in the glare and roar of the car, he regretted what he had done, and called out to the Miracle Man.

There was a screech of brakes.

After the man had finished shouting and driven off, he trudged down the hill.

There was only one place to go now, and that too was dangerous. They would be out looking for him, and Seb might well guess where he had gone, and come for him alone. And no one would be surprised later to hear that the unstable midget boy, who suffered from fits and had run off in so wild a manner, had had an unfortunate accident and been found by his elder brother.

Dead.

Or maybe not found at all.

That, too, was possible. He did not know what kind of death Seb had planned for him tonight. Or whether the plan would be different tomorrow.

Tomorrow. But first he had to live through tonight.

At least the roads were quiet. He turned right at the bottom of Somerville Gardens and wandered along the top of the Undercliff, then cut down toward the bridge over the railway line.

The smell of the estuary was reassuring, but he looked around him as he walked, watching for shadows. Nothing stirred. Maybe it was later than he'd thought. Maybe it was tomorrow already. He crossed the bridge and made his way along the Cinder Path, the water on his left silky and still and bright under the moon. At the gate to the dinghy rack, he stopped and looked over the slumbering hulls, then pushed it open and hurried to *The Miracle Man*.

I've got to talk to you.

He leaned close to the mast and stroked it.

I'm so scared.

A sharp creak of timber nearby made him jump back. But all he saw was a deserted rack, and the shining surface of the estuary. He rested his head against the mast.

I don't want to die, Miracle Man. I want him to die.

He heard another creak and jumped back again. But as before, there was no one in sight. For a while he stood motionless, listening to the *pink! pink! pink!* of the halyards knocking against the masts as the breeze caught them. Then he bent down to the mast once more.

I'm scared of dying. And scared of killing. I'm even scared of miracles.

Especially miracles.

He hurried to the stern and tried to ease off the cover, without undoing the lanyard. But something was wrong. It was tighter than when he had left it. Still looking around him, he loosened the lanyard enough to fold the cover back from the starboard quarter.

In the stern of the boat lay a dead cat.

Its limbs were mangled, its neck crushed by some huge grip. He felt his stomach heave, struggled to the edge of the rack, and vomited into the water.

Another creak of timber made him whirl around. This time he was certain Seb was there.

But still he saw no one.

He took the body of the cat, left it on *Scorpion*'s foredeck, then hurried back to *The Miracle Man*, slid into the cockpit, and forced the cover back over the edge. Breathing hard, he crawled over the thwart and centerboard case, squeezed around the mast, and burrowed under the foredeck.

It was comfortingly dark, and the buoyancy bag made something of a cushion. He closed his eyes, wondering about Dad.

And Seb.

And what lay ahead.

Somehow he drifted into sleep, and for a while escaped thoughts of death. But during the night something woke him: a noise, or the slight chill that came with the dew, or just his own fear, he didn't know. He stared into the blackness, uncertain at first of where he was, knowing only that he was afraid. Then he stiffened.

Footsteps.

He froze and listened.

They approached and stopped. Then started again, slowly circling the hull.

He'll find me, Miracle Man. He'll—

They had stopped again, close by the mast. He held his breath through what seemed an endless silence. Then he heard the sound he had dreaded, the light tap of the lanyard toggle against the side of the boat.

The cover was being loosened.

He tried to calm his thoughts, think what to do. But he knew he was caught like a mouse in a trap.

A hand shot through the opening and lunged at him.

He shrank back against the curl of the bow, as the fingers, so horribly familiar, loomed toward his eyes.

Suddenly, to his surprise, they stopped, an inch from his face, and began to feel their way around the inside of the hull.

Aware of a tiny hope, he twisted his head away from them,

praying they would not touch him, praying the cover would not come off. Slowly the hand withdrew, and he breathed out with relief.

At once it reappeared, darting like a snake's tongue around the centerboard case in search of its prey. He thought of the dead cat and wondered whether Seb would feel around the stern to see if it was still there.

If he hadn't already seen it on his own boat.

But the hand withdrew, and a moment later the footsteps receded.

When dawn came, he climbed out of the boat and gazed across the mud to where the waters of the Ray flowed, gray and calm, toward the eastern sky. Then he tightened the cover and made his way to the gate.

The body of the cat was gone.

He hurried along the Cinder Path and through the silent streets until he reached the house he had never called his home. He pulled the spare key from under the plant pot, let himself in, and went straight to his father's room.

And Dad stood up from the chair, dropped the bottle to the floor, and held him.

ten

They ate breakfast in silence. Dad fumbled with the napkin holder, looked this way, that way, half stood up, sat down, then fumbled with the napkin holder again.

Seb sat quietly, eating.

Watching.

Midget caught no glance, but he knew the eyes were on him, following his every movement. He lifted the mug to his mouth, and felt the eyes watch him do it. He drank the coffee, and replaced the mug. And felt the eyes watch that, too.

He looked up sharply. But saw only a face averted. When he looked down again, he felt the eyes return.

Dad spoke at last.

"Don't go out in *The Miracle Man* today. I know it's the Midsummer race. Stay at home this time."

He looked up and wondered how he could refuse, without hurting Dad anymore.

"It's not that—you know." Dad's face was pleading. "I mean, you've proved to us you can sail. And win races. No question about it. Right, Seb?"

Seb continued to look down at his food, as though intent

only on that. But he answered, in a quiet, even voice.

"Right, Dad."

The false cheerfulness was gone; in its place, a new, quiescent tone. Dad would not feel the danger within it, the rage of a will frustrated and focused more intently than ever on its objective.

"It's just that . . ." Dad stood up and walked over to the window. "We were worried sick about you last night, weren't we, Seb?"

The eyes were now openly on him, with Dad's back safely turned.

"Right, Dad."

"Worried sick. We looked everywhere for you. Seb even went out twice, didn't you?"

"Right, Dad." The eyes held him, like those of a cat, watching a prey it knows it will get in the end; waiting for the parent to leave it, just for a second. Then Seb stood up.

"Think I'll be off."

Dad turned around sharply. "Already? But it's only—"

"I'm seeing Ned. And I want to do some tuning before the race."

"Oh." Dad looked helplessly at each of them in turn. "I just thought, maybe today . . ."

"See you later, Dad."

Dad's eye flickered toward the floor, then back to Seb.

"Okay!" he said cheerfully. "No problem. See you later. I'll . . ." The voice faltered. "I'll see you later."

Seb opened the back door and walked out into the passageway.

Dad called after him. "You're all right, aren't you, Seb? I mean—you sound a bit—"

"Fine, Dad. Just tired."

"Tired! That's it. Tired after last night." Dad's head nodded mechanically. But his face showed only confusion.

"Right," said Seb. "Tired after last night."

"See you later, then."

"Okay."

The back door clicked shut. Midget stared down, unable to look at the weary, worried face any longer. He wished he could explain that he had to go to the race, too, had to know where Seb was at all times, had to be with *The Miracle Man.*

Because being with *The Miracle Man* was the only chance of safety he now knew.

Dad came over and sat next to him; then stood up again almost at once, wandered through to the living room, and closed the door behind him. Midget closed his eyes tight.

He knew what his father was doing.

He stood up and walked through the hall, and waited outside the living room door until the sound of crying had died down, then opened it and walked over to the sofa. Dad looked up and simply raised his arm. Midget slid underneath and closed his eyes again.

He wondered, as he felt Dad's body shake, why he couldn't cry, too. But for once his own tears seemed far away.

He waited several minutes after Dad had stopped, then looked up. The eyes were calmer, but still dark and inward-looking. He thought for a moment, then reached out and started to dig in Dad's trouser pocket close by.

"Wrong one." Dad's voice was expressionless, but this old ritual might still help.

He sprawled over his father's lap and thrust his hand into the other pocket. Now he felt the cigarettes. He pulled the packet out, put a cigarette in his own mouth for a joke, then placed it in Dad's. Then he went back to the pocket.

"Wrong again. Shirt pocket."

He took out the box and sorted through the matches, tutting in mock seriousness as he did so.

"I know, I know. I shouldn't put the dead ones back."

There was more warmth in the voice, more life, even amid the sadness. He found a live match and struck it. Dad dipped his head just enough to light the cigarette, then leaned back with a sigh, the exhaled smoke curling up toward the ceiling. Midget burrowed under his arm again.

They sat in silence for a long time, and somehow he forgot about Seb, and death, and the boat. Until Dad spoke.

"Go on. Win me another race."

But when he saw the boat, it was his turn to cry.

The decking, thwart, and centerboard case, even the outside of the hull, were covered in scars.

A knife had been at work.

He whirled around in anger, searching the waterfront for the enemy he knew had done this. And there was *Scorpion*, only fifty yards from the slipway, with *Raider* close by.

Furiously he rigged and launched the boat, and raced after them toward the starting line. He had no picture in his mind, no plan or goal, only a rage he had never known before, which conquered fear and thought.

Ahead, he saw *Scorpion* and *Raider* turn to face him.

So it's open war, Miracle Man. They don't want to race.

They want my blood.

He saw them break apart, like dancers in formation, Ned luffing seaward, Seb jibing around toward the shore. Midget bore down on the gap between them.

Suddenly they turned and closed on him like hounds.

He stiffened, trying to think what to do. He had right of way over *Raider*, but Ned showed no signs of changing course as he raced in on port tack. Seb surged toward him from inshore on a fast reach.

Both boats would hit him amidships.

He thrust the helm down to bring *The Miracle Man* to

starboard and try to slip past *Raider's* stern. Instantly Ned bore away, jibed full circle, and tacked onto a new course to cut him off.

Desperately he checked the gap. It was wider now, maybe wide enough to squeeze through.

But Seb had read his mind and was already bearing away to keep downwind of him.

He looked for support. But all the other boats were at the start. And he knew that to anyone watching, this was just a game. Three boys having fun.

He heard the five-minute gun. It seemed to dare him to try and reach the starting line.

He jibed and raced in closer to the shore. Ned bore away and shadowed him, keeping downwind, then luffed and charged in again. Seb luffed, too, and the two boats shot toward him, like the points of an arrow.

He stared at the diminishing gap and knew he wouldn't make it. Angrily he luffed to avoid a collision, heading now for the shore itself. Seb went about at once, and tracked with him.

They're mad, Miracle Man. They're mad.

He saw them grin at each other. Anger welled deeper within him. *The Miracle Man* plunged toward the seawall.

He looked quickly around him. Seb had edged closer, leaving him no room to jibe back on his earlier course. There was nothing else to do but to go about.

He drove the helm down, threw himself across the other side of the boat, and made ready to lean out. To his dismay, he found the hull drifting backward.

The mainsheet had snapped.

He snatched the end of the rope. It was meant to look frayed, but he could see it had been cut, just enough to let him sail for a while and then be caught on the water.

119

"Something wrong with your boat, Mad Midget?" Seb's taunt rang out close by. "Better hurry up and mend it or you'll drift into the shore."

Seb went about, raced past the bow, and bore away with a laugh toward the starting line. Ned followed, grinning inanely back at him.

He glared after them in desperation, wishing he could reach out and pluck them back. *The Miracle Man* bumped against a moored dinghy. He grabbed hold of it with one hand and lowered the sail with the other; then, still gripping the gunwale of the moored boat, he looked for Seb and Ned again.

At first he saw two boats. Then one.

Seb's boat.

He's the one, Miracle Man. He's done all this. He's got to be stopped. If I had a gun, I'd–

The picture flashed into his mind so sharply that he felt he had switched on a screen before him. He tightened his grip on the dinghy, narrowed his eyes further, blocked out all other thought. As through a tunnel he saw *Scorpion's* shiny hull and bulging sail, and Seb himself, smugly leaning back; his task done. He squeezed his eyes closer until they almost shut.

The edges of the tunnel tightened, the image within still clear, as in the telescopic sight of a gun. The picture in his head danced wildly, begging for release. He mentally squeezed the trigger.

A savage exhilaration gripped him as he felt power shoot over the water. The surface of the estuary seemed to redden, like the water in the vase of flowers that day at Dr. Patterson's. But he was too excited to dwell on that now.

"G-get . . . h-him!"

At once *Scorpion* rounded into the wind, the sail flapping.

He saw Seb put the helm up to bring the boat back on course.

That won't work, brother!

He quickly changed the picture. Immediately *Scorpion* responded, this time bearing away in the other direction, Seb floundering around the stern as he tried vainly to control a tiller that was no longer his.

Midget laughed, his anger quelled in the delight of power. Today it was stronger than ever. He looked into the picture, and mentally moved Seb's tiller again.

Scorpion shot back into the wind, throwing Seb to the lee side of the boat. Now *Raider* had turned and was racing back, Ned peering in amazement at the antics of his friend. Midget waited until the two boats were close, then changed the picture again.

Scorpion swung to leeward so fast that Ned barely had time to alter course to avoid collision. He saw the two of them shouting at each other.

Now it was a game. Now it was fun. Power over Seb was the best miracle he could ever have wanted. He let his mind play with the picture, making *Scorpion* turn this way and that like a puppet. Suddenly Seb stood up and turned toward him.

He could not see the expression on his brother's face at this distance. But something told him Seb had sensed the source of power.

For a moment Seb simply stood there, gazing toward him, just keeping his balance as the boat yawed back and forth. Then he jerked his hand up in the middle-finger gesture.

The fun vanished; the fury returned. The picture seemed to change of itself, though he knew it was his will that fashioned it. Through the tunnel, the telescopic sight, all movement quickened. *Scorpion* shot into the wind, throwing Seb to the lee side of the cockpit. Then, just as sharply, the bow skewed around the other way.

Seb struggled toward the center, his body caught in the twisting motion of the hull. The bow tore around to starboard like a dog chasing its tail.

Seb ducked, knowing the jib was coming. Too late.

The boom swung in like a hammer and struck him in the face. Arms whirling, he crashed over the side.

Midget gasped, momentarily shocked at what he had done. *Scorpion* shivered into the wind and capsized. Seb's body, stunned and motionless, floated off with the tide.

The fear grew that this was wrong. He felt he could hear Old Joseph's voice inside his head, telling him so. But still he wanted death.

An engine roared nearby and he saw the rescue dory racing toward the body. Ned was already near, his arm outstretched to pull Seb in. A man had set off from the shore in a dinghy and was rowing furiously to join them.

He felt the pictures in his mind clamor, hungry for the food of his will.

Suddenly the rescuers were having difficulty. The engine of the dory spluttered inexplicably and threatened to die. *Raider's* sail shivered, the wind suddenly against it. The man in the rowboat, who had looked so capable, had somehow lost an oar over the side and was having to scull around to pick it up.

Miracle Man, stop it. Old Joseph didn't want this.

But the pictures were creating themselves within him, unrolling like a tapestry in his mind, the will to destroy life stronger than the will to save it.

It's wrong. It's murder.

First my mother. Now my brother.

Help me.

A new picture slipped into his mind, of a funeral, with lots of people standing around the coffin, all wearing black. Ned was among the mourners. Dad was making a speech.

Jenny was crying.

The madness seeped from him and he saw with relief that the boats were under control now and once again hurrying toward the body.

Ned was there first. Seb shuddered as he was dragged clear of the water, and vomited over *Raider*'s foredeck. The dory arrived, and the crew hauled Seb on board, then headed off to take care of *Scorpion*. The man in the rowboat backwatered and stood by, watching.

Midget turned away.

Relieved. Disappointed.

Confused.

He pulled out the paddle and drove *The Miracle Man* back to the dinghy rack. As he reached the slipway, he heard the starting gun go off.

But he no longer cared about races.

For a moment he saw Jenny's face again, still crying at the funeral; then the image darkened and vanished, as though drowned in the tide that swirled over him like a flood of fear.

He sat on the seawall, staring down. Below him the rocks were cooling, now that the late afternoon sun was less fierce. Close to his feet, a line of dry seaweed marked the high point of the tide a few hours before. Already the water was beyond the base of the rocks and creeping back over the mud. He looked out toward the Ray, wishing he could have stayed afloat and sailed there instead. Two more days and the tides would be perfect for Ray-Days.

But two days ahead was too far to think.

There was no pleasure in seeing Seb taken to the hospital.

No victory. No relief.

Only confusion. About death, about power, about what was right.

About what he wanted anymore.

He looked at the dinghies a few yards out on the running moorings. Still just afloat. But they would be high and dry before long. He put his hand on the bollard close by and fingered the rope, following it down with his eyes into the water, where the weeds trailed from it like dusky hair.

Angrily he tugged at the line. Twenty yards out, the little dinghy at the end jerked forward a foot, then fell back with the ebb. He stood up and picked his way down the slope, feeling step by step each of the slippery rocks. Losing his balance, he groped for the line, missed, and found himself sprawled on a slimy coat of weeds. He pulled off his shoes and socks, threw them up the seawall, and stepped down to the water.

At first the weeds cushioned his feet from the nubs of rock, then he felt the shingly stones and squashy bed of mud. He cupped his hands over his brow and gazed out to sea.

I thought I wanted to kill him, Miracle Man.

And you nearly let me do it.

Damn you.

He slumped in the shallows and let his head drop to his knees.

When he awoke, the water was gone.

His body ached. He had a crick in his neck. He was cold.

Toward the Ray a haze hung over the mud. He looked for boats and saw only shapes. Then he sat up in alarm.

Seb was standing a few hundred yards out.

Looking toward him.

He stiffened. But Seb's at the hospital. He can't be here.

Still the figure stood there, unmoving, too far out for the features to be clear, yet instantly recognizable. He remembered the figure he thought he had seen from above Chalkwell Station, and the fuzziness around his brother's body that time in the garden. A shiver ran through him.

He forced himself to stand up. There had to be an explanation. Slowly, deliberately, he set out over the mud toward it.

He kept his eyes down on the clusters of shells dotted around the mud and plodded on, determined not to look up even once, until he had reached the spot where the figure was. As he walked, he told himself that Seb must have been let out of the hospital already, that the accident hadn't been very serious after all, and he'd decided to walk out to the Ray for a swim.

He glanced back at the shore. It seemed so remote he could hardly believe he lived there. He ducked his head again and hurried on across the mud.

With every step, the urge to look up grew stronger.

Miracle Man, I've got to—

He raised his head at last.

The figure was gone.

He darted glances in every direction, at bait diggers, at bathers wandering out to the Ray, at a man scraping barnacles off his boat.

Then he saw it again.

Inshore. Where the Leigh swimming pool used to be.

Unmistakably Seb.

He trembled slightly. It was impossible for anyone to move so far in those few minutes. But he no longer knew what was impossible.

He hurried toward the bridge, this time keeping his eyes fixed on the figure, with its blurred, uncanny outline. He could feel himself walking faster, forcing the pace, driven despite his dread to get there, and find out what it meant.

A hundred yards to his right, he heard a train rumble past. He locked his eyes more tightly onto the figure. This time he wouldn't look away, not even to check the ground before him. He heard his bare feet squelch in and out of the mud, felt them cut themselves on the upturned shells he dared not look at to avoid. He remembered his shoes on the seawall and told himself they would have to wait. Suddenly he felt one foot sink into the mud and stick.

With a groan of dismay, he toppled over.

He was up in a second, his eye scanning the shore.

The figure was gone again.

He spun around, madly searching. Further along the Cinder Path, a tall figure was striding toward Chalkwell Station. He plunged forward. Then stopped.

That's not him, Miracle Man.

Another figure caught his eye, striding the other way.

Again he plunged forward. And stopped.

Don't be stupid, Miracle Man. That's not him either.

He tried to study the passersby on the Cinder Path, but now the holiday-makers, dogwalkers, lovers, stroller pushers, none of whom he had noticed before, seemed to swell into a huge, gloating face.

At last he saw the figure again.

Further down the Cinder Path, moving toward the dinghy rack.

Suddenly he was running. Fear clawed at him, but he thrust it aside in his rage to reach the figure. Water spattered his thighs; shells grazed his feet as he charged in to the seawall. He scrambled up the rocks to the Cinder Path and sprinted toward the rack.

At once the crowd enveloped him. Now it seemed a monster with countless forms, all holding him back. He pushed forward, dodging, squeezing, but the throng seemed to build up like breakers on a beach, driving him back. He ducked his head and forced his way through, gauging his way from the feet all around him.

Suddenly the path opened up.

Twenty yards in front, he saw the figure, still striding ahead.

It was Seb. It had to be Seb. Horrible, mean, loathsome Seb. It couldn't be anyone else.

But Seb's at the hospital.

He lunged forward, arms groping for contact. As though sensing his presence, the figure stopped, and looked around.

He drew back, his chest heaving, and saw two eyes leveled on him like the barrels of a gun.

Then the stranger turned and continued his walk toward the rack.

He made his way back to the running mooring and collected his things, then slowly crossed the bridge and climbed the pathway to the road.

I'm going mad, Miracle Man. Or maybe I've always been mad. Maybe Seb's been right all this time.

But when he looked back over the estuary again, he saw the figure standing there still.

eleven

Dr. Patterson peeled away the last of the wires.

"Well done. An excellent morning's work," he said, and had already begun to walk toward the door that led back to his office before he realized Midget had not followed.

He came back and looked down. "Is something wrong, young man?"

Midget hardly saw him. He was remembering how tired and almost frightened Seb had looked when he had come home from the hospital late last night; how he had gone straight to bed without a word. The psychiatrist coughed, pulled up a chair, and sat down.

"Tell me about it."

Midget frowned. Inside his head he could hear all the words he wanted; he could almost touch them, they seemed so solid. But when he opened his mouth, barely a growl came out.

The psychiatrist watched him for a moment, then stood up. "I'll just get my secretary to make your father a cup of coffee."

Midget reached out at once. "P-p–" He found he was gripping the doctor's sleeve, and made himself let go.

Dr. Patterson sat down. "It's all right, young man. Take your time. I'm not going anywhere."

"P-p-p–" It was coming. He twisted in his chair, fighting the stampede of words in his head, determined to force out the one he wanted most. "P-p-pow-er."

The psychiatrist frowned. "Power? Is that what you said?"

He nodded eagerly.

"I'm not . . . quite sure . . . what you're asking," said the psychiatrist. "There are various types of . . . power." He pronounced the word with some hesitation. "Physical power to move things, for example. Lift things up–"

Midget shook his head violently.

"Not that? Well, then there's mental power. Ah! That's the sort of power you mean, is it?" The psychiatrist smiled. "All right, we have mental power, certainly. We–"

"C-c-con-trol . . . th-th-ings–"

"Control things? Mentally, you mean? Well, yes, if you like. You demonstrated that this morning. And the last time you came. You made the red light change, by mental power. And–I must say–you seem to have picked up how to use your mental power in this respect more quickly than anybody I've ever known."

The psychiatrist paused. "Quite uncanny, actually," he said. "You have an ability to control your brain waves that I have never seen before, in anyone. And I notice you are acquiring power in other ways. You are managing to speak a little more, and your nervous mannerisms have diminished. And your father tells me there have been no further attacks recently. Is that correct?"

Midget nodded.

"So to sum up, we could say that these are examples of mental power—mental control—over things. Am I getting near to answering your question?"

Midget leaned forward. "P-p-p—" He found his head nodding with each sound, as though it wanted to print the word on the psychiatrist's face. "P-p-peo-ple . . ." he said finally. "P-power . . . over . . . p-peo-ple."

He wiped the saliva from his mouth.

The psychiatrist stroked his chin and frowned again. "Power over people? Well, you could say we have power over people in the sense that we can persuade them to do things. And they can persuade us to do things. Then they have the power, of course. That's especially true of those who are closest to us. Is that what you mean?"

Their eyes met.

"No, it's not what you mean." The frown deepened. "What you must be referring to, then, is the power of thought alone."

The measured voice stopped, as though reluctant to pursue the subject.

Midget thought of Old Joseph, as he so often did these days, and wished he were here now, jabbering and gibbering in his funny old way, with that crazy lopsided cap. And for a strange moment the room almost felt like the boatyard, with its chains and ropes and wood shavings, and clamor of work. And the old man's restless eyes.

The psychiatrist spoke again. "I don't know whether you're really asking me about . . . black magic." The voice wavered slightly, then hurried on. "Some people do claim they have power over others in this way. Or that others have power over them. It's not something psychiatrists pay much attention to." He smiled quickly. "It's certainly nothing for you to worry about."

Midget closed his eyes, and murmured, "S-S-Seb." And as he spoke, he saw his brother in his mind, and suddenly realized that they both had power over each other, different kinds of power; and he no longer knew whose he feared more.

In the darkness of his closed eyes, he heard the words stutter from him, like a disembodied voice.

"Am . . . I . . . m-mad?"

The psychiatrist broke in at once. "Of course you're not mad. You mustn't say things like that."

Still he kept his eyes closed. The darkness seemed more friendly than the light. He heard a scrape as the psychiatrist pushed back the chair, then the voice again. "Come on, young man, snap out of these negative thoughts. You should be full of optimism at the progress you're making, instead of sitting there all slumped up, looking like some kind of wraith."

The words sprang at him. He sat up in alarm, eyes wide open, a confused memory crashing around his mind.

The psychiatrist was smiling. "That's better! A touch of energy!" But the smile quickly vanished. "What is it?"

He didn't know. He only knew that one of the words frightened him, that he was trembling, and wanted to run.

Again he thought of Old Joseph. And suddenly he knew the word, and remembered the old man as he lay dying in the boat, the mad, misty eyes glazed as a windless sea; and he remembered how the word had frightened him then, even though he didn't know what it meant.

If you want a bad miracle—an' you see it good—an' you believe in it good—then you'll get it. Only somethin' else comes with it.

Evil comes with it.

An' evil comes before death. Like a wraith.

That's what the old man said.

131

"Wr-wr-wrai-th—" he stammered.

He felt the psychiatrist touch his arm.

"I do apologize, young man. I just wanted to shake you out of your negative mood. But it wasn't perhaps a very kind word to use in the circumstances."

"Wr-wra-th . . . w-wha-wha?" He gripped the chair tight.

The psychiatrist watched him uneasily. "Are you . . . are you asking me what a wraith is?" he said slowly.

He felt his head nod up and down like a hammer.

"I see." The psychiatrist adjusted his tie. "Well, I don't want you to attach too much importance to what I just said." He coughed. "But, yes, all right, a wraith is—I suppose—some sort of ghost. Er . . . perhaps that's the best way to define it. It's . . ." He paused. "Well, hold on. Let's look it up for you. Then we'll know exactly."

He hurried to his office, clearly glad to be moving, but was soon back, a large dictionary in his hand.

"Now then." The voice was calm again, under control. "Let's see what we can find." He flicked through the pages, found the one he wanted, and ran his eye down the columns. Midget felt his mind race back to the estuary, to the figure he had seen, and to Old Joseph.

Evil comes with it.

An' evil comes before death. Like a wraith.

"Here we are! I'll read it to you." The psychiatrist was trying to sound cheerful. "'Wraith: a ghost or apparition, in particular the apparition of a person living or thought to be alive, supposed to appear around the time of his death.'"

He closed the book with a thud, and smiled.

"My definite apologies to you, young man. It was unquestionably the wrong word to use to describe the way you looked." He laughed and began to make a joke against himself.

But Midget no longer heard or saw him. The smiling face seemed to fade, like an apparition itself, a thing of no substance. As if through a mist, he saw the door open, and another ghost figure appeared, dimly recognizable as his father. And the two ghost figures stared down at him in silence.

He closed his eyes tight to blot them out.

But instead of darkness, a third ghost figure appeared.

Standing on the mud as before.

twelve

So the figure means death, Miracle Man.

Seb's death.

The Miracle Man slid out through the early morning stillness on the last of the ebb tide. He settled himself on the windward side of the boat and tried to conjure the pleasant feeling of anticipation he usually had when setting out for a Ray-Day. But he knew this Ray-Day was not for pleasure. It was for solitude.

For thinking. Though already he disliked the course of his thoughts.

The apparition of a person living.

The words came back, just as the psychiatrist had read them from the dictionary yesterday.

Supposed to appear around the time of his death.

He checked over the side of the boat for depth. A few feet below, he could see the muddy bed slipping past, and for a moment wondered if he had left his departure from the rack too late.

Just ahead was the deeper water of the Creek, and he

debated whether to follow it until it joined the Ray, or chance his luck and cut across the bank. He checked over the side again.

Okay, Miracle Man, if you say so. We'll try the bank.

At that moment the bottom dipped away; seconds later it returned, and the Creek was past. The centerboard caught the mud and bounced up a few inches.

He leaned forward and raised it slightly, cursing his decision to go this way.

But *The Miracle Man* was moving, the water chuckling under the bow with the sound he now often heard in his thoughts, even when far from the boat.

The centerboard jumped up again. He felt a jolt under the hull, and the bow skewed to starboard. He pulled the board up further until it cleared the mud, then brought the bow back on course. It was lucky he didn't need much board down, with the wind northwesterly and not too strong. He gazed out at the line of fishing boats moored in the Ray and the crowd of sails already there.

He had expected them, even though the tide was rather early for a Ray-Day. With a drought as bad as this, the Ray was an obvious sanctuary. They'd be walking out from the shore later, the moment the mud was uncovered.

He wished he could have it to himself.

The Miracle Man drew closer to them. The mud bank below the hull seemed higher, but it was slipping past steadily, and the centerboard had not touched for some time. A couple of hundred yards and he would be there. He looked back at the shore, almost a mile astern, and felt a sense of release.

At last the water darkened and the bow broke into the Ray.

He pushed the board full down, hauled in the sail, and altered course toward Two Tree Island. Everywhere he saw sailing dinghies and cruisers, and power boats of various sizes, all waiting, as he was, for the mud banks to show on either side of the channel.

He saw a spare mooring buoy to port, jibed around and picked it up, and made fast. Then he lowered the sail, sat in the bottom of the boat, and waited.

At least he ought to be left to himself out here, with Seb out with Ned again, and Dad at work. Yet the unease remained, and he found himself studying the figures around him.

Gradually the mud banks defined themselves, glistening at first as the tide drew back but soon hardening under the sun. Before long the South Bank was littered with people, running, splashing, shouting.

He hoisted the sail and cast off the buoy, happier to stay afloat despite the teeming craft, and sail up and down the Ray. And as he sailed, he wondered about Seb.

Then he saw her.

She was wandering out from the shore, unmistakable with her hair streaming in the wind, and the jeans, rough-cut into shorts, which she so often wore, to Margie's dismay. She walked slowly, almost as though she had meandered this way by accident without realizing where she was going, though he knew that was ridiculous. Suddenly she waved.

It couldn't be to him. He looked around him, expecting to see someone else nearby.

But there was no one.

Now she was laughing. He hauled his wind and steered toward the bank, trying to think of what he should say.

At least she's not a ghost, Miracle Man. That's something.

She waded out to meet him and caught the bow.

"Hi! Hope I'm not interrupting your sail."

"N-n–"

"It's really strange," she said. "I was stuck at home, arguing with Dad. Just for a change. And–you won't believe this–I just couldn't stop thinking about *The Miracle Man.*"

He dropped his eyes under the intensity of her gaze.

"I couldn't get the boat out of my mind. And Dad and I were having this fight, and I got really mad, and then Mom kicked me out and told me to walk it off, and–"

She lowered her voice, and he had to lean forward to hear her against the flapping of the sail.

"I got this feeling I had to walk out to the Ray. It's crazy. I never walk out to the Ray. I hate sloshing over mud and shells and things."

He noticed that her face had clouded, and it was a moment before she spoke again.

"Something made me come out. I kept thinking of *The Miracle Man,* and . . . I just had this feeling you'd both be here." She giggled. "Sounds funny, doesn't it, saying 'you both'? Like *The Miracle Man's* alive, too." She shivered. "It's cold. Can I get in?"

He fumbled with the tiller, not knowing where to look. "Y-y-yes."

She climbed aboard, dripping, and he steered back into the channel. For a while she sat silent, gazing toward the pier, then she turned and smiled back at him.

"How long before the tide comes in again?"

"F-f-fo-four–"

"Four hours?"

He nodded.

She shook the hair from her face. "Is there any way you could put up with me until then? I'd love to sail back to shore with you. I mean, if you didn't mind."

He dropped his eyes again, and nodded.

137

"And when the tide comes back, can we be the last people on the South Bank before the water covers it?"

And he nodded again.

He soon realized she didn't want to talk or go ashore, only to sail for hour after hour. They headed down to Two Tree Island, then back along the Ray to the Low-Way Buoy and out to the pierhead. Here the wind was fresher, but they drove on for another mile through choppier seas to the deeper waters of the estuary, where the tankers plowed up to London or away toward the North Sea.

By the time they returned to the Ray, the flood was well under way, and most of the South Bank was gone.

She spoke for the first time in over an hour.

"You come out here to think, don't you? And get away from everything."

He picked a thread of seaweed from her hair and dropped it over the side. She watched him and smiled.

"It's a good place to think." She looked away suddenly, frowning toward the horizon. Then she spoke again. "I did really badly in the violin competition."

She fell silent once more, as though debating whether to continue. But then she went on, in a quiet, musing voice.

"I wanted to do the Mozart. I love it, I can play it really well, but—" She pursed her lips. "My violin teacher made me do the Brahms, and he knows I hate it. And it's nowhere nearly as good as the Mozart." She blushed. "Sorry. I shouldn't throw all this at you."

"O-Okay—"

She gave him the hint of a smile.

"You're a good listener. Dad wasn't. He was a pig."

Again she fell silent, and he thought she had finished speaking. But to his surprise she went on, her voice even slower, even more reflective.

"After the competition my teacher said I played the Brahms without a single mistake. Phrasing good, tempo good, you name it, I did it right. I asked him what I did wrong. You know what he said?"

Her eyes seemed to look not at him but back into herself.

"He said no matter how well you act a part, your true feelings always come out in the end. Even though I played the piece really well, my hatred for it still came out."

She stared down at the water gurgling past.

"He said it's easy to give yourself to what you love. But you have to give yourself to what you hate, too. You have to sacrifice the part of you that hates until you love what you once hated. Whatever its faults."

He looked into the sky, and for a moment thought he heard thunder.

The mud was shrinking fast. Inch by inch the channel widened as the flood nibbled the banks. Most of the boats had set sail, and several were gathered around the mouth of the Creek, waiting to edge back to shore.

"Come on," she said. "Before the South Bank goes."

They sailed in to what was left of the mud. *The Miracle Man* grounded, and Jenny got ready to jump over into the shallows. To his amazement, a picture sprang into his mind.

Clear. Complete. Urgent.

"S-s-stop!"

She looked back at him in confusion, and he pointed over the side. She drew back in disgust.

"A jellyfish! One of those horrible ones. I'd have jumped right onto it."

She looked around at him suddenly. "How did you know it was there? You can't see it from where you're sitting."

He looked down, hoping she would not press him to speak. Then she said, "You've changed so much since *The Miracle Man* came into your life."

They waited for the jellyfish to float past, then jumped into the shallows and rammed the anchor in as deep as it would go. Then they raced to the middle of the island of mud.

For some minutes they stood there in silence, watching the water close in around them. Suddenly he felt her hand on his arm.

"Are you all right? You keep looking around, like you're expecting to meet someone. Here of all places."

He shuddered, unaware of what he had been doing. But he managed a nod.

"Just as well we've got *The Miracle Man*," she said. "Seeing as neither of us can swim."

He felt the water trickle under his feet as it swallowed the last inch of mud. A hundred yards from them, *The Miracle Man* was afloat again, swinging at anchor as though eager to depart.

"I know," she said. "It's time to go home."

As they walked up Woodfield Gardens, she pointed ahead.

"Looks like no one's back at your place. Windows closed, no car. Do you want some tea with us?"

He thought of Ben and Margie and shook his head. Phony laughter and clucking insincerity were the last things he wanted right now.

"You're doing it again," she said suddenly. "Looking around you. You've been doing it all day."

He flushed, but she only smiled.

"Thanks for letting me sail with you. I really enjoyed it.

Better go in and make my peace with Dad now. If I can sacrifice the part of me that hates, that is."

That was it, Miracle Man. That's what the violin teacher said. Sacrifice the part of you that hates until you love what you once hated. Whatever its faults.

"Thanks again," she said and was gone.

He walked over to his own house and up to the front door.

Sacrifice the part of you that hates. Until you love what you once hated.

He entered the house, closed the door, and walked down the hall toward the kitchen.

Love what you once hated. Whatever its faults.

The footstep behind him was brief. The blow that followed knocked him unconscious.

thirteen

Pain roused him.

But only to a world of blackness, confusion, fear. His body was bouncing, rolling, twisting. He was being carried, roughly, like a bag of garbage.

He opened his eyes and saw blackness still. Something was over his head, some kind of rough cover, tied around his neck so that it chafed as he moved. Every part of him seemed to throb. He started to wriggle and shout.

Instantly he was thrown. Something soft and wet cushioned his fall, and he smelled mud. Before he could think, a boot crashed into his face, and he plunged back into unconsciousness.

From then on, he knew little, except the shadows and half shadows of his mind, as it wandered in and out of reason, wanting only death. He had ceased to be carried, that much he knew. He was being dragged through mud.

And he must be struggling because of the kicks that still rained upon him, though their pain no longer touched him.

Then he realized he had stopped. He was lying shivering,

sodden, in some unknown place, the chafing hood still tight over his head.

Suddenly he was shouting, in a voice he barely recognized as his own. Shouting for death and life at the same time.

He heard the squelch of footsteps, plunging and sucking closer, closer. A hand seized his neck and squeezed in a gesture all too familiar. The voice in his ear was chillingly casual.

"So here we are to put you out of your misery for good. Just like I always promised."

It moved around to the other side of his head, and went on conversationally.

"I hope you weren't too uncomfortable in the trunk of Ned's car."

He struggled to break free, but the hand around his neck tightened until he gasped for air. The voice slid around to his other ear.

"I'll be back later to dig a nice big hole. But you won't see me." It dropped to a whisper. "You'll be dead."

A blow crashed into his head and he lost consciousness again.

The first new thought was of darkness.

Where am I? the thought asked.

But there was no memory, no feeling to give a clue.

A second thought came.

Pain.

There was pain, I remember it.

I remember it? Who's I?

No answer came. Only a third thought.

I'm dead. Aren't I?

A chill chased the thought away. Suddenly there was feeling, of mud, water, wind.

A body trembling.

By some will of its own, the head turned this way and that as the eyes searched in vain for something other than blackness. A blackness that grated the face as it moved.

The sack, the makeshift hood.

Memories tumbled back, and with them the pain. Every muscle seemed to ache, every breath to hurt. His head throbbed as though a hammer pounded inside it. He twisted wildly from side to side, trying to free himself from the grip of the hood, but he could feel it was roped there. He tried to reach for it and felt his arms jerk backward.

He hadn't realized he was tied up.

Panicking, he tried to stand. But ropes around his neck and thighs kept him on his knees. He felt water creeping around his waist.

He thrashed his head against the hood, writhed and wriggled, strained at the ropes with all his strength, water splashing over his stomach and chest.

Suddenly he saw a pinprick of light. The sack had slipped, and there was a tear, a tiny gap, close to his eye. He strained toward it and squinted through.

One glimpse was enough to make him sink back in despair.

It was a light from the shore. About a mile away.

He knew where he was now, and that this was the end. Gazing through the gap in the cloth, he saw the piles of the pier rising above him, the bracings crisscrossed like the bars of a cage. He saw the dark underside of the planking, and a few hundred yards to seaward the jutting edge of the pierhead.

The moonlight flickered on the flooding waters as they edged toward the shore, and deepened around him.

He yanked his arms against the ropes, though he knew it was useless. Seb knew too much about knots to make any mistakes. He floundered backward with the recoil of his own efforts and felt the cold metal pile with its barnacles and weeds between his shoulder blades.

If I have an attack now. If—

He tried to think rationally but already his limbs were stirring of their own accord, ready to burst out into violent movement.

Calm. Keep calm.

Through the gap he saw the moonlit water stretching toward the Ray. Even now he found himself pondering its beauty, remembering how often he had watched the flood tide claim the mud, as it was soon to claim him.

Calm. Keep calm. Don't black out.

He slumped back against the pile. Suddenly it seemed like a large, slimy finger; he squirmed forward, his skin prickly with revulsion, but the ropes restrained him again. The hood slipped and he lost the gap.

Once more, blackness enveloped him and into it came the shrouded memory of Old Joseph. For the first time in all his confusion he remembered the Miracle Man.

At once his mind seemed to clear. Pictures poured into it, one by one, gradually merging into a single image, which he adjusted as he had done so many times. The chilly water now felt warm and relaxing like a bath. The wiry cords around his body seemed like strands of cotton draped almost playfully over him.

The pile, which had seemed so slimy and soggy, hardened and narrowed. The barnacles on it sharpened and glistened like blades. He began to move his body up and down, letting the rope rasp over them.

He could hardly believe how calm he felt, how much in control. Up and down, up and down, and with every movement, the ropes in the picture seemed thinner, the barnacles sharper.

Up and down, up and down. In his mind he saw no ropes at all now, only blades slashing. Suddenly he fell forward and felt the water splash against his body.

All calmness vanished in the ecstasy of freedom. He scrambled to his feet and tore off the hood. An infinity of stars burst upon him, the moon glistening in their midst like a polished ball, in contrast to the gaudy lights of the shore.

He threw off the ropes and waded toward the land, the water now above his waist. But still it felt warm and soft. He dipped his hands and caressed the surface.

You're not my enemy. You're my friend. The Skipper.

The water teased his skin with a sparkling phosphorescence.

I know who my enemy is.

At last he overtook the advancing tide and stepped ahead onto clear mud. Only then did he turn and stare back through the darkness to where he had been.

I know who my enemy is.

The new picture formed of itself. There was no need to will it into being, or change it, or add to it. It unfolded under the direction of the sole emotion he had left.

Hatred.

He dimly remembered the walk home, the fussing and fawning on his arrival, the doctor, the police, the endless questions, none of which he answered.

And Seb. Seb had more questions than anyone, and they were written in his eyes. But Midget no longer worried about Seb.

Seb would soon be dead.

fourteen

The picture was the most powerful he had ever known.

For two days and nights it had unfolded before him, like a film he had seen time and time again yet never tired of watching, though he knew its every detail. And now he was ready to see it acted before his eyes.

The Miracle Man foamed out from the shore, scything the crests with ease as the bow rolled toward the Ray. Under him the hull quivered like a beast ready for the hunt. He looked for Seb and Ned and saw them off the starboard quarter, sailing close together as though they wanted to talk.

But neither seemed to be speaking.

It occurred to him that this was Seb's first sail since the day he was knocked overboard by the boom. He looked into the picture again.

It would be his last.

The sail shivered and he adjusted the sheet. The wind was gusty and unpredictable, just as he had pictured. Nothing could go wrong.

He looked back at them again. There was something strange about Ned. The puffy face had lost its leer and the eyes seemed to mirror some inner conflict. He even seemed uneasy with Seb.

Seb had kept his distance since the escape from the pier. His face had retained its composure. But the smile was gone.

Midget shrugged. It didn't matter anymore.

Seb was finished.

The Ray drew closer, the water sparkling in the sunlight, and everything just as he had drawn it in the picture. Cruisers, dinghies, speedboats, water-skiers, just as he had seen in his mind. In a dream he turned *The Miracle Man* down the channel toward the mooring buoy that he knew would be waiting for him, untouched by anyone else, as the picture decreed.

There it was, bobbing astern of the anchored ketch, which he had also pictured in his mind.

He picked up the buoy and secured the boat, then lowered the sail and lay down in the bottom of the boat. Looking up at the sky, he saw the bungee flutter this way and that under the caprice of the wind. He closed his eyes, the picture brilliant within him, and waited.

Two hours later, he sat up. The mud was high on either side, the South Bank crowded with swimmers, but his eyes moved quickly to the channel, searching for *Scorpion* and *Raider*.

There they were, sailing up the middle, just as planned.

He hoisted the sail, cast off the buoy, and raced toward them, scanning the mouth of the Ray for the next link in the chain of images he had created.

Then he saw it.

The monster rumbled past the Low-Way Buoy, its hideous body rolling as it splashed toward them. The cabin rose high above the water, the two aerials at the top quivering in the air. The dinghy in the stern davits swung over a boiling wake.

It was just as he had wanted. At least forty feet long, doing a good twenty knots, with an owner too arrogant to slow down or alter course for anybody.

He searched for the fat man in the yachting cap he had seen in his mind. And there he was by the wheel.

For a second he felt a tremor of fear at what was unfolding before him, but he thrust it aside at once. It was too late to change now.

Seb must die.

He hauled in the sail and raced toward the monster. The gusts were growing stronger, the wind direction more fickle. A capsize now would destroy everything. He threw his weight out to balance the boat.

The monster bore down on him, teeth snarling with foam. He watched, fascinated by the mountain of death he had created, reveling in the fear on the fat man's face at the little boat apparently set on a suicide course. The bow yawned above him like a lion's mouth.

He held on another second, two seconds, three seconds. Then tacked clear.

The monster roared past, only inches away.

The man thrust his head out of the window and bellowed down at him. But he took no notice. His eyes were already on Seb and Ned.

It was all so easy now. Just as in the picture, they were running dead before the wind toward Two Tree Island. Just as in the picture, Ned luffed away from the path of the monster powering up behind them. Just as in the picture, Seb stayed on course to let it pass to starboard.

See it good, want it good, believe in it good.

He looked into the picture and felt the wind direction change.

Now, Miracle Man.

At once the wave smashed into *Scorpion's* bow, buffeting it to leeward. The wind, already behind the sail, hurled it across in a violent jibe.

Seb ducked and threw himself inboard. But he was not quick enough. The boom thudded into his head and he fell back to port, dropping the tiller. The boat rounded to starboard, out of control.

The monster struck amidships and drove him under.

Midget squirmed around the boat, unable to keep his body still. All he could see was the picture below the surface, the picture he had dreamed and desired and believed in.

Of propellers.

Slashing, slicing.

Slaying.

Kill him, Miracle Man. Kill him.

The mast and sail broke the surface at the stern of the monster, then the wreckage of *Scorpion's* hull.

And Seb's body, face down.

The fat man threw the engines full astern. The monster bridled to a halt, foam fizzing about the hull like the mouth of a rabid dog. A woman rushed up from the cabin and flung a life preserver toward the body.

But the body didn't move.

Midget heard a sail close by, and saw *Raider* sweeping in.

"Quick!" shouted Ned. "Come and help!"

But Midget hauled his wind and, without a backward glance, sailed off toward the open sea.

It was over.

It was early evening when he returned. The tide had flooded the banks long before, and was now ebbing once again in its endless cycle. But he had hardly noticed the tides.

He had been far out to sea.

Not once had he looked back, even at the sound of the

150

helicopter fluttering to the scene of the accident. He had known the fat man would radio for help.

And that it would do no good.

The open sea had beckoned, and he had followed, seeking the solitude he needed in which to rejoice.

But now, so many hours later, as he neared the slipway, he wondered why his heart was so full of pain.

The figure appeared in the corner of his eye as he bent over the hull at the base of the slipway. For a moment it seemed to freeze, remaining dark and amorphous; then suddenly it moved, and he breathed out with relief.

It was only Jenny.

She didn't come down to him, but walked away, along the top of the rack, and he wondered if she was angry with him for not trying to help Seb, and disappearing when he was needed. Ned must have told everyone about it. He pulled the hull clear of the water and walked up the slipway.

She was sitting on the planking at the end of the rack, where *Scorpion* used to be kept. He hesitated, then walked down to her.

She didn't look up.

"He's slipping away fast." There was no anger in her voice. Only sorrow. "They just kept him alive somehow, on that stupid man's boat. Till the helicopter got there. He's in the hospital now. On a life support machine." She frowned. "One of the propellers sliced into his head."

He thought of the figure lying just as he had pictured, in the twilight between life and death.

"He's going deeper into the coma. The doctors say he could come out, but they're not hopeful. It's like . . . it's like some power's holding him back from getting better. Forcing him into death."

He heard a rumble of thunder far away.

"Your father's got to decide tomorrow afternoon whether to switch off the machine."

He turned away and gazed at the sky darkening over the estuary. Her voice came again, small and hesitant.

"You've . . . you've got some part in this. I just know it. There's something you've got, some power you've discovered—since *The Miracle Man* came."

He looked at her sharply, wondering what she knew, what she felt. What she wanted.

She met his eyes for the first time.

"That time he called you Midget. That wasn't a joke, like he said. Was it?"

He shook his head.

"And those scratches on your boat, did he—?"

He nodded.

A tear had strayed down her cheek. She wiped it away angrily.

"I know he's done something terrible to you. Maybe lots of things. I only started to feel it a few weeks ago." She sniffed and wiped away another tear. "He was always telling everybody how much he cared about you and wanted to help you. We all believed him. Then that day he called you Midget—" She sniffed again. "I suddenly saw the fear in your face when he came toward you."

She stared at the planking again. He half reached out to touch her shoulder, but she turned sharply toward him again and he pulled his hand back.

"Does he hate you because your mother died giving birth to you?"

He nodded.

She was silent for a while. Then she said, "Well, whatever he's done, he must have paid for it now. The doctors think his brain's probably damaged, and even if he survives, he'll never be the same again." She looked at him through narrowed eyes. "But he's not going to survive, is he? Unless you let him."

He leaned over the rail and stared at the water.

So she knew. He wasn't surprised. She had worked out so much already. And she had always understood him better than anyone else.

He heard *The Miracle Man* sail clap as a gust caught it. The storm would not be long now. The rain would come and soon everything would be different.

She touched him on the arm. "You'd better put *The Miracle Man* away and get back. Your father might be home now. And he'll need you."

She started to go, then suddenly turned to him again.

"You can't let him die. He must have paid the price, for whatever he's done to you. Forgive him. Sacrifice the part of you that hates, remember?"

He watched her wander away down the Cinder Path, and even after she had disappeared from view, continued to gaze after her, half hoping she might return and speak to him again. But he knew she would not.

Forgive him. Sacrifice the part of you that hates.

The picture of the figure in the hospital bed filled his mind, as clear as when he had first formed it, desired it, believed in it. And the darkness he had put there grew deeper, as his will worked upon the figure, squeezing its life away.

But all of me hates him, Miracle Man. He's done too much for me to forgive.

The thunder rolled once more in the distance.

It was after midnight when he heard footsteps outside his room. So many times he had dreaded footsteps at night. But never again. The door swung open, and he saw Dad standing there.

"Thank God you're here. I thought you might have run away."

153

Dad came in and sat on the bed, his face hidden in the darkness.

"I can't stay long. I've got to get back to the hospital. But I must talk to you."

The thunder rolled again, and it was longer, louder, deeper.

"I know about the pier. And some of the other things. Ned's father came to the hospital. Said Ned's been acting strange the last couple of days. Well, tonight he broke down. And the story came out."

Midget sank back, unsure of his feelings.

"Ned's been taken in by the police. The officer in charge called me at the hospital. They're going to want to speak to both of us, and Seb, too, obviously, if he–" Dad breathed out hard. "And I got a letter from Dr. Patterson after you left for the Ray."

Lightning blazed outside the window, illuminating the features of the room with a cool glow before darkness plunged back.

"He wants to do some experiments on you. Thinks you may have some mental power you're just starting to discover. Says you tried to talk to him about it." Dad paused. "But that's not all."

The wind had started to moan now, and rain was drumming against the window.

"He said you were very distressed when he mentioned Mom. He thinks you may be suffering from guilt about what happened." Dad leaned closer. "It wasn't your fault. She'd have wanted you to live in her place. And if she'd lived, she'd have loved you just as much as I do."

Midget gazed up at the ceiling, and wondered whether her eyes were peering at him through the darkness right this moment. He had sometimes felt that during the night.

Lightning flashed again and he jumped. Dad held his arm to steady him.

"He said he saw fear in your face when he mentioned Seb." His father lowered his head, and his voice. "Seb was close to Mom. Too close. He was a quiet boy, wouldn't say boo to a goose. When you were born and she died, I thought he'd go into his shell. But he didn't. He changed. Made loads of friends. Did well at school, sports, everything. Got that confident manner. Christ! I never thought he could—"

Dad broke off and gazed toward the window, not speaking for some time. Then he turned back.

"I can't bear to think of him dying. I know he deserves to be punished. But I'd give anything to see him live. Anything."

Once more Midget thought of the darkness closing over his brother. And he realized there was a darkness over him, too.

And it came from his heart.

"Try and forgive him," said Dad. "Whatever he's done."

Forgive him. They keep asking me. First Jenny, now Dad. But they don't know how much he's hurt me.

"I've been praying for a miracle," said Dad. "But I'm not very good at it. You're the only one who seems to make miracles happen around here."

He remembered the words of that crazy old boatbuilder he had known so little and loved so much.

Some folk are real good at miracles. They can make 'em 'appen right away.

The thunder came again, and seemed closer still.

"Maybe we're not meant to make miracles happen," said Dad, as though he had heard Midget's thought. "Maybe it's all down to fate."

There's good miracles an' bad miracles. So make sure the Skipper's 'appy with what you want.

155

Dad stood up slowly.

"Better get back. Go and see Margie and Ben in the morning. I'll phone them with any news. They'll probably all be coming to the hospital anyway. I know Jenny's in a state."

Jenny.

Jenny says sacrifice the part of you that hates.

But all of me hates. All of me wants him to die.

Dad kissed him on the head.

"You get some sleep. You've been through enough already."

Once more the lightning flashed, brightening Dad's face for a moment. His father leaned down.

"The storm'll pass. I promise."

Midget felt thunder rolling inside his head. But at least he knew now what he had to do.

"Forgive me," said Dad.

And Midget smiled up at him, one of his very best smiles, though he knew Dad could not see it.

"G-good-b-bye," he replied.

fifteen

Late in the afternoon the doctor called them together.

"Well, this is quite something for the books. I didn't expect him to come out of the coma, as you know. But—" he looked around at them all. "It seems miracles exist after all."

"When can we see him?" said Dad.

"Can they do anything about his face?" said Margie.

"Is there brain damage?" said Ben.

Jenny gazed out of the window toward the estuary and said nothing.

The doctor waited for them all to finish.

"There may be brain damage. It's too early to say. As to the face . . ." He shook his head. "Plastic surgeons can do a great deal these days. But in this case . . ."

"Will that be for life?" said Margie.

"I'm afraid so."

Dad stepped forward. "I've got to see him."

The doctor stopped him. "In a moment, yes. But before I take you through, I have to tell you he appears to have developed some kind of speech impediment. He can only form parts of words, and even then with the greatest difficulty. And there's another thing."

He paused, frowning.

"He's clearly in considerable distress. And he keeps trying to say something. It's hard to understand the words, but one of the nurses is convinced he's asking someone to forgive him for something."

Jenny looked around sharply. "Who's he asking to forgive him?"

The doctor shook his head again. "It's difficult to make it out. But it sounds like—Joseph. Does that make any sense?"

Dad sighed. "Yes, it does. Does anyone know where Joseph is?"

Jenny turned back to the window. "I do," she said.

He looked around at the water closing upon the South Bank.

So here we are, Skipper. You and me and *The Miracle Man*. All together. For the greatest miracle of all.

The anger of the storm was gone, and only the rain was left.

But the rain is my friend, Skipper. It keeps people away. When I need you to myself.

The hull was floating again as the incoming tide lifted it from what was left of the mud.

I can't forgive him, Skipper. I can't find a picture stronger than the one in my head. And that's the one that's killing him.

I should have talked to you, Skipper. Not the Miracle Man.

He looked around him again, still searching.

Then he saw it.

The figure of Seb, standing at the seaward end of the bank, gazing toward him.

He pulled out the big hammer he had taken from the

garage, swung it high above the hull, and brought it down with all his strength.

The topside split with a crunch. He lifted the hammer and brought it down again, and again, and again.

Water seeped in over the bottom boards.

He wiped the tears from his face, tore out the mast and boom and threw them into the sea, kicked off the transom flaps, punctured the buoyancy bags. Then he leaned his shoulder against the bow and pushed.

At first, nothing seemed to happen. Then the tide took his burden, and he stood back, breathing hard, and watched the remains of *The Miracle Man* float slowly away.

He turned back to the figure.

It stood in the same place like a statue in the sea. He walked toward it and stopped on the last patch of mud.

This time you won't move. This time I've beaten you. Seb will live.

Then he realized the figure had changed.

It was no longer Seb's face that he saw.

It was his own.

He felt the water caress his feet.

For a while he stood still, enjoying the peace and beauty of the estuary, and the warmth of the rain on his face, and wondering why this moment, which he had feared all his life, no longer frightened him.

Then he smiled, and walked through the shallows toward the figure and the deepening sea.